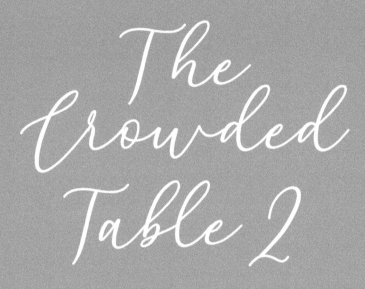

The Crowded Table 2

THE FATHERHOOD ADVENTURE

56 Men Share Their Stories

ANGELA CONNELLY
WITH MEGAN McDANIEL & MANOLA SECAIRA

The Crowded Table 2: The Fatherhood Adventure
First Edition, 2023
Copyright © 2023 by Angela Connelly

To order additional books:
www.amazon.com
www.angelaconnelly.com

ISBN: 978-1-952943-23-2

Softcover Version ISBN: 978-1-952943-24-9
Ebook ISBN: 978-1-952943-25-6

Editorial and Book Packaging: Inspira Literary Solutions, Gig Harbor, WA
Book Design: Brianna Showalter

Printed in the USA

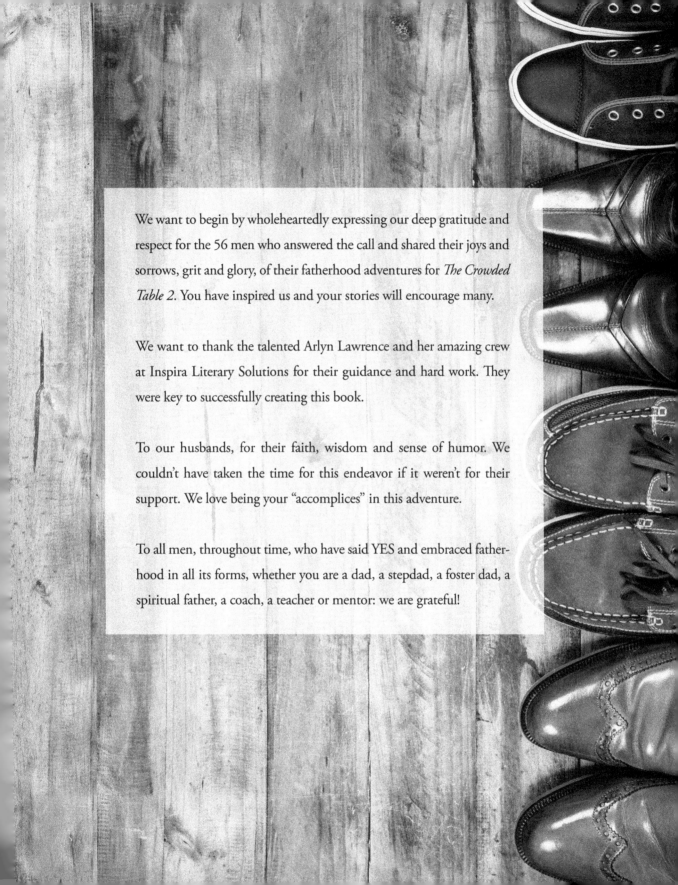

We want to begin by wholeheartedly expressing our deep gratitude and respect for the 56 men who answered the call and shared their joys and sorrows, grit and glory, of their fatherhood adventures for *The Crowded Table 2*. You have inspired us and your stories will encourage many.

We want to thank the talented Arlyn Lawrence and her amazing crew at Inspira Literary Solutions for their guidance and hard work. They were key to successfully creating this book.

To our husbands, for their faith, wisdom and sense of humor. We couldn't have taken the time for this endeavor if it weren't for their support. We love being your "accomplices" in this adventure.

To all men, throughout time, who have said YES and embraced fatherhood in all its forms, whether you are a dad, a stepdad, a foster dad, a spiritual father, a coach, a teacher or mentor: we are grateful!

If—

Rudyard Kipling (1865-1936)

If you can keep your head when all about you
Are losing theirs and blaming it on you,
If you can trust yourself when all men doubt you,
But make allowance for their doubting too;
If you can wait and not be tired by waiting,
Or being lied about, don't deal in lies,
Or being hated, don't give way to hating,
And yet don't look too good, nor talk too wise:

If you can dream—and not make dreams your master;
If you can think—and not make thoughts your aim;
If you can meet with Triumph and Disaster
And treat those two impostors just the same;
If you can bear to hear the truth you've spoken
Twisted by knaves to make a trap for fools,
Or watch the things you gave your life to, broken,
And stoop and build 'em up with worn-out tools:

If you can make one heap of all your winnings
And risk it on one turn of pitch-and-toss,
And lose, and start again at your beginnings
And never breathe a word about your loss;
If you can force your heart and nerve and sinew
To serve your turn long after they are gone,
And so hold on when there is nothing in you
Except the Will which says to them: "Hold on!"

If you can talk with crowds and keep your virtue,
Or walk with Kings—nor lose the common touch,
If neither foes nor loving friends can hurt you,
If all men count with you, but none too much;
If you can fill the unforgiving minute
With sixty seconds' worth of distance run,
Yours is the Earth and everything that's in it,
And—which is more—you'll be a Man, my son!

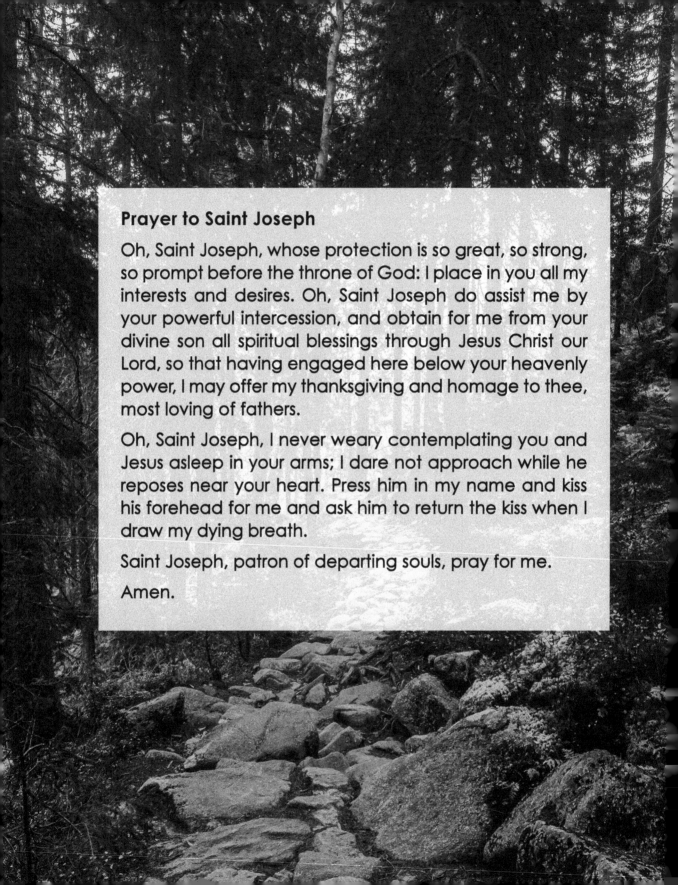

Prayer to Saint Joseph

Oh, Saint Joseph, whose protection is so great, so strong, so prompt before the throne of God: I place in you all my interests and desires. Oh, Saint Joseph do assist me by your powerful intercession, and obtain for me from your divine son all spiritual blessings through Jesus Christ our Lord, so that having engaged here below your heavenly power, I may offer my thanksgiving and homage to thee, most loving of fathers.

Oh, Saint Joseph, I never weary contemplating you and Jesus asleep in your arms; I dare not approach while he reposes near your heart. Press him in my name and kiss his forehead for me and ask him to return the kiss when I draw my dying breath.

Saint Joseph, patron of departing souls, pray for me.

Amen.

This picture of St. Joseph has hung above my (Angela) husband's dresser for 30 years. He has been inspired by St. Joseph's fatherhood throughout the good and bad times of raising our nine children…through midnight 103-degree fevers, through whooping cough quarantines, through desperately trying to find out where a teenager was at 2:00 a.m., through nights filled with labor pains and nights before weddings…

Joseph's calmness leads the way, in every situation. His love and devotion teach beyond words. His fatherly actions show us all how to love Jesus and one another. That's why *The Crowded Table 2: The Fatherhood Adventure* is dedicated to St. Joseph, and to every man throughout time who spiritually, emotionally, or physically:

- Protects the vulnerable
- Provides a home
- Teaches children
- Guides the lost
- Dries the tears
- Supports the struggling
- Gives a hand
- Welcomes the prodigal
- Comforts the sorrowful
- Encourages the anxious
- Gives direction to the wandering
- Has used his gifts talents, energy, to be the hands and feet of Christ

"For I was hungry and you gave me food to eat…
Whatever you did for the least of these you did for me."
(Mathew 25:35-40)

Table of Contents

Foreword

In many places, the traditional family does not receive the respect it should. One way to make a positive contribution showing the need for the particular gifts that fathers can offer is to hear from fathers. *The Crowded Table 2: The Fatherhood Adventure* does just that. These stories manifest how fathers can embrace their calling to guide and protect their families. It encourages men that they do not need to be perfect in order to be good fathers. The example of so many fathers striving to fulfill their essential role in the family will inspire us all.

My own experience of fatherhood is complicated, but I have been blessed to recognize what it is to be a good father. My birth father abandoned me and my seven siblings when we lived in Belfast, Ireland. My mother brought all eight of us to Canada for a new lease on life. She did not experience that new start, because she was killed in a car accident on Christmas Eve. Out of tragedy, I discovered fatherhood.

When the eight O'Reilly children were

left orphaned, my loving uncles and aunts agreed to take the children. Given their own circumstances, some could accept a boy, others a girl; some could even accept two of us. But Dorothy and Ed O'Reilly could not see a family divided. They agreed to adopt all eight of us, and thereby added to their own four children so that we became a family of 12 children. That is how I learned about fatherhood.

My adoptive father was in every way

a father. As St. Thomas Aquinas teaches, God has adopted us. He did not generate us, but He chose us so that we might be perfected. Ed O'Reilly wanted what was best for all his children, his own offspring and those he adopted. And what was best? The truth! He taught us to respect revealed truth and the truths that we can discover. He taught us the crucial importance of integrity, reliability, and hard work. In so many ways he taught me to be a father.

That does not mean that I have suc-ceeded in being a good father to my own 12 children. However, my children are remarkably good, no doubt because of their wonderful mother. This much I know: do not abandon your children. As a father, you must know what is true and what is good. Present the true and good to your children, and let God do the rest. But to be a good father, you must have a wife who perfects you, improves you, and inspires you. That is why St. Joseph is the patron of fathers. Our Lady perfected

Joseph; she improved him, and he received every inspiration from her.

St. Thomas Aquinas has a wonderful commentary on the prayer that Jesus taught us. Who could imagine that, when we pray to God, we can address Him as "Our Father." It is Jesus who gave us the confidence to address the Creator of the Universe as our Father. Thomas Aquinas explains that we can say: "Our Father..." because God cares for us as a father should. He adds that God does not want to be regarded as a master, and He does not want to treat us as servants. He calls us to be His children. He intends to be a father to loving children.

Here is what we find to be the challenge for fathers: we might have skills, but we need the help of others; despite our weaknesses we must be confident because our trust is in God; we must be teachers and therefore we must come to understand what is true; despite our failures we must inspire and not discourage; we must be caring and attentive to our children. Only then will we be good fathers.

I have known Angela Connelly since we were students at Thomas Aquinas College. Now I work with her closely as she serves on the board of governors of her alma mater. Her dedication to her faith, her country, and her family is apparent in all that she does. This second book in the *Crowded Table* series continues her legacy as someone devoted to finding powerful witnesses for the beauty of the family.

Dr. Paul J. O'Reilly
President, Thomas Aquinas College

"Your greatest contribution to the kingdom of God may not be something you do, but someone you raise."

– Andy Stanley

Preface

One of my seven sons called and said, "Mom, you've got to listen to this…it's your song! It's called 'The Crowded Table' by the Highwomen."

He was right! It WAS my song! As I listened, tears rolled down my cheeks…

"I wanna house with a crowded table…"

I listened to the song probably 50 times and then felt a call to do more…to write *The Crowded Table* books, to celebrate family, community, belonging, serving one another, embracing home and children, accepting the vulnerable…with "a place for everyone by the fire," as the song goes—in a world that values self above all else.

The crowded table lifestyle—the crazy, chaotic, unconventional adventure of kids, family, and community—can make you pretty countercultural. Loving the sometimes disrespected but the abundant lifestyle of embracing "the crowded table" is an adventure.

In our hurting world that struggles with isolation, despair, mental illness, and depression, maybe family and community provide a way forward to bring healing, purpose, and peace. Maybe women and men who embrace the crowded table have something of value to share. Maybe there's joy in the chaos and peace in community.

While worldly success, empowerment, and independence are good things, without the context of giving, service, community, and family they are empty and meaningless. *The Crowded Table* books, and the patchwork quilt of the 52 women and 56 men's voices, flip the cultural lie of "self above all else" right on its head.

In *The Crowded Table 2: The Fatherhood Adventure,* 56 diverse men vulnerably and humorously tell it like it is. They've been through it all. They are the dads, the mountains, the streetlights that are all imperfectly perfect, as the lyrics in "The Crowded Table" describe—and so very needed in our lost world to show us the way home.

In the song, "The Crowded Table," the last verse talks about sowing the seed, planting happiness, letting roots run deep, and that when it's love we give, it's love we reap.

I couldn't agree more.

So let's sow the seed, let's nurture the roots, let's plant love and happiness and belonging. Let's celebrate motherhood and fatherhood and laying down our lives in all the ways we are called to bear fruit. It's a mission, an adventure, and we are all equipped by the grace of God, the true author of our being, the Heavenly Father who shows us the way.

So sit back, be ready to laugh, relate, be encouraged, and enjoy the wild ride into the adventure of men who commit to family, love, life, and sacrificial leadership.

~Angela Connelly

Introduction

Our broken world desperately needs fathers.

Our culture does not necessarily respect the importance of the gift that men who embrace fatherhood bring to the table. In fact, our children, our families, our culture, and our world are experiencing a "fatherlessness crisis." Homelessness, mental health, delinquency, drug abuse, suicide…the statistics are all escalating in children from fatherless homes.

Men, your leadership, love, guidance, and strength are vitally important and they are gifts only you can uniquely bring to the table. Are you ready for the most challenging exciting mission you will ever face?

The Crowded Table 2: The Fatherhood Adventure is a quilt of male perspectives on the experience of raising children—the vulnerabilities, uncertainties, purpose, fun, craziness, and joy of it all.

Fifty-six real fathers from around the world, Guatemala to Canada, and throughout the U.S., tell it like it is. They all are imperfectly striving and failing and striving again to lead and guide and love their children, their students, and their businesses, wherever their own crowded table calls them to lead.

There is truly a father-shaped hole in the heart of every human. There is a deep craving for safety, protection, guidance, and love, and the reassurance that all will be well. Men, you are equipped to lead and protect and help not only your kids and wives, but the world. As the Scout motto goes: "Be prepared."

As my co-author, Megan McDaniel, wrote, "Maybe you have a father whom you miss, a father whom you love, or one who needs your forgiveness. Maybe you never knew your father or your father was abusive or unkind. Maybe he was a living saint and you judge yourself inadequate as if you will never measure up. The great news, my friends, is that He is calling you by name too. He is calling your name and longing to tell you about your life in light of eternity. He is whispering in the gentle wind of a

1

summer breeze and sometimes as loud as thunder about His love and plans for you. He longs to have you step into the rich inheritance of His eternal plan of life and sonship for you." While every human falls short, we can look to our heavenly Father as the true and perfect source of all love and protection and guidance. It's a big job, but you men are equipped with the power of grace to live out that heroic call.

For *The Fatherhood Adventure* book, I asked two dear friends, both who contributed essays for the *The Crowded Table: The Brave and Beautiful Choice to Mother Many,* to write along with me. They both love the crowded table. Both know deeply the value that fathers bring to the table.

Megan McDaniel and husband Tim have six children.

Manola Secaira and her husband Antonio are the parents of eight children.

My husband Jack and I are the parents of nine children.

So, do the math: we three busy moms together have 23 children!

As you know, when you ask a busy person to do something, it gets done.

SO...sit back and enjoy! Hear the stories from 56 real dads, all the mountains and the valleys, the failures and the triumphs, and why "the crowded table" is the best, most meaningful adventure you'll ever experience.

~Angela Connelly

Science Speaks

"For the best part of thirty years we have been conducting a vast experiment with the family, and now the results are in: the decline of the two-parent, married-couple family has resulted in poverty, ill-health, educational failure, unhappiness, anti-social behavior, isolation and social exclusion for thousands of women, men, and children."
- Rebecca O'Neill, *Experiments in Living: The Fatherless Family*

Our culture today diminishes the role of fatherhood. It's almost as if the sign says, "Fathers need not apply." This attitude is destructive and false. Let's take a look at its devastating consequences.

In his book, *Becoming Dads: The Mission to Restore Absent Fathers*, author and fatherhood advocate Marvin Charles writes,

"Many experts agree that almost every social ill faced by America's children is related to fatherlessness. Children from fatherless homes are more likely to live in poverty, become involved in drug and alcohol abuse, drop out of school, and suffer from health and emotional problems. Boys are more likely to become involved in crime, and girls are more likely to become pregnant as teens. If fatherlessness were classified as a disease, it would no doubt be a certifiable epidemic worthy of attention as a national emergency."

It's evident that science proves over and over again the absolute need and vital importance of fathers to the thriving of children, families, and culture.

Today, 40 percent of children are raised without a father in the home. The statistics are staggering for children from fatherless homes: 90 percent of all homeless children

"A little science distances you from God, but a lot of science brings you closer to him"
- Louis Pasteur

3

are fatherless, 63 percent of teen suicides are fatherless, and 85 percent of teens and children with behavioral and mental health challenges are fatherless. Moreover, fatherless families are 25 percent more likely to raise children in poverty.[1]

Science also proves the incredible advantage that children have when a father is in the home:

- they do better at school
- they have more confidence
- they understand human relationships better
- they develop fearlessness and courage from the active play and wrestling that many fathers engage in with children

Further research shows why fathers matter. A University of Bristol study shows that 50 percent of girls whose fathers leave home when they are five years old or younger are more likely to have mental health challenges when they are in their teenage years. According to the study, they are also more likely to develop physical health problems as well.

Another study, from Professor Anna Sarkadi at Uppsala University, shows that having an engaged father reduces psychological problems as well as reduces delinquency from school.

In a 26-year-long longitudinal study from 1990, it was proven that the number one factor in developing empathy in children was the father's engaged involvement. Fathers spending regular time with their children translated into children

"I build molecules for a living. I can't begin to tell you how difficult that job is. I stand in awe of God because of what He has done through His creation. My faith has been increased through my research. Only a rookie who knows nothing about science would say science takes away from faith. If you really study science, it will bring you closer to God."

– James Tour, *American Chemist and Nanotechnologist, Professor of Chemistry, Materials Science and NanoEngineering*

becoming compassionate adults. Overall, more than 80 percent of studies on father involvement and child well-being, published since 1980, have found a direct relationship between positive father involvement and child well-being.[2]

Finally, although the science is much more exhaustive, engaged fathering is associated with more positive moral behavior in children, according to research by the University of Pennsylvania. The studies show children who feel warmth and closeness with their fathers are twice as likely to enter college, 75 percent less likely to have a child in their teens, 80 percent less likely to be arrested, and 50 percent less likely to show signs of depression.[3]

Dads: the children NEED you! Science proves it!

~Angela Connelly

1 U.S. Census Bureau 2020
2 Rohner, Ronald and Veneziano, A., "The Importance of Father Love: History and Contemporary Evidence," *Review of General Psychology*, 2001.
3 Ibid.

MARVIN CHARLES

Marvin Charles is the founder and executive director of Divine Alternatives for Dads Services (DADS) in Seattle, Washington. For over 20 years, he and his wife Jeanett have been effectively helping men reclaim their positive role as the fathers their children need. He is also an ordained minister and an emerging national leader in confronting the fatherlessness crisis, and helping communities create and support stronger fathers and healthier families. Marvin and Jeanett have a blended family of eight children, and are the grandparents of five. *www.aboutdads.org*

Breaking the Cycle of Fatherlessness

When I speak to groups around the US about the devastation that fatherlessness is causing in urban America, I equate it to the AIDS virus. AIDS doesn't kill in and of itself; what it *does* do is break down a person's immune system and make the individual susceptible to infections. Infections are what kill an AIDS victim. In the same way, a father's absence from the home opens up the family to all kinds of destruction, including the "symptoms" just mentioned.

Many people today do not understand why fatherlessness is such a threat to children and families. That's because we've been programmed to look at the symptoms of the problem—whether they be juvenile crime, unwed pregnancies, drug addiction, or gang violence—rather than the cause.

Fatherlessness goes beyond the boundaries of race, culture, and socioeconomic status. It has tremendous, exponential effects on our culture at large, especially as it plays out in the life of a child and in the development of his or her identity. It renders that child highly susceptible to negative peer influence and poor life decisions, including drugs, out-of-wedlock pregnancies, and criminal behaviors. And, crucially, it is a cycle that perpetuates itself from one generation to the next.

Children who go down these life paths often do so in an ill-fated attempt to fill the void left by their absent fathers. They seek love, comfort, and security, but they do so inappropriately, ending up with more children like themselves, conceived not out of love, but out of a need to be loved. As ill-equipped parents, they try to raise these children without a job or money, many of them continuing their drug habits and leaving their children in a state of dire need, sometimes even outright abandoning them. Without any real, lasting intervention, the cycle continues and expands—unless an individual does what it takes to stop it.

We can point the finger all over the place at whom or what is to blame for the current state of affairs. The reality is that it's a perfect storm of a number of factors. And the only way to turn it around is by restoring absent fathers to their children.

> "We repeat what we don't repair."
>
> – Toby Mac
> #speaklife

One of my favorite verses in the Bible comes from the life of Joseph, in the Old Testament. Having risen to a position in Egypt second only to Pharoah himself, Joseph reveals himself to his brothers who, years earlier, callously left him in a desert well to die. He tells them, "As for you, you meant evil against me, but God meant it for good, to bring about that many people should be kept alive as they are today" (Genesis 50:20). Whether the predicament in which a man finds himself as an "absentee father" is of his own making or the result of circumstances beyond his control—such as being born into a fatherless family—or a combination of both, every man still has a choice to turn to God and follow "divine alternatives," not only for the good of his children and their children, but also for the good of the community.

When a father leads his four-year-old son down a crowded street, he takes him by the hand and says, "Hold on to me." He doesn't say, "Memorize the map," or, "Take your chances dodging the traffic," or, "Let's see if you can find your way home." The good father gives the child one responsibility: "Hold on to my hand." God does the same with us.

No matter how bleak a situation a man finds himself in, he can turn his life around and become a committed, involved father. The confidence I have about this is based upon the evidence of countless men—myself included—who have overcome many obstacles in order to build a better future for themselves and their children. Men who knew me in my former life, or who get a little glimpse of my story, will feel, *Wow! If this guy could turn things around, I sure can!* My story, which you can read in my book, *Becoming Dads: The Mission to Restore Absent Fathers,* illustrates that "God doesn't call the qualified but rather qualifies the called."

Breaking the Cycle

A sign hangs prominently in our DADS office: "And he will turn the hearts of the fathers to the children, and the hearts of the children to their fathers, lest I come and strike the earth with a curse." (Malachi 4:6).

This last verse in the Old Testament speaks of the very real "curse" of fatherlessness that we are seeing in our nation. We can see what the effect of this curse looks like, as well as the consequences it has on children, mothers, family units, and society at large. But is there a way to stop it?

I believe there is, but it isn't just a question of changing policy or instituting more social programs. I believe "reversing the curse" is a matter of the human *heart* changing, starting with the father toward the child and then the child toward the father.

At DADS, we've seen men's hearts soften and turn toward their children. We've witnessed them overcoming huge obstacles to reconnect with their children and become involved, responsible fathers. When this happens, a generational curse of fatherlessness down family lines begins to be reversed, and a beautiful legacy of fatherhood begins. We have seen this happen in countless families, including my own.

Fatherlessness does not need to be a dominant trait in the DNA of American families. It *is* possible to break the cycle—and every father who connects with his children, and commits to being the dad they need, changes not only the life of that child, but of a community, a generation, and our society as a whole.

PART 1

The Adventure of Fatherhood

Fatherhood is by far the greatest adventure in life! Courageously venturing into the unknown. Sometimes scary, sometimes exhilarating, always worth it!

In our family, with seven sons in a row between our two daughters, we are always up for adventure, ready or not. One spring break, my husband Jack and I decided to surprise our seven children (the two youngest weren't born yet) with the World's Greatest Road Trip.

As we pulled up to our house after school, there, in our driveway, was the most beautiful sight our kids had ever seen: a huge mobile home with a large "RENT ME" sign covering a painting of the Grand Canyon.

Yep…we were going on an adventure!!!

Their little eyes nearly popped and they all screamed with delight! The neighbors even came out to watch. (Even though they were used to the noise of our Connelly clan, they knew something special was up.)

As the kids swarmed the RV, Jack was sitting in the driver's seat with the biggest grin of all. The five oldest climbed in, and there were our two littlest babies, sitting in their car seats, strapped in and ready for takeoff. I had packed each child a backpack…and we were off.

Those were crazy days and full of adventure. Before we were married, my husband had kayaked the Yukon and backpacked through Europe, and he was bound and determined to bring our kids on memorable experiences—every single wild adventure was worth it!

For two weeks we were free, self-contained in our little womb of family—very cozy with nine humans smashed together in a camper, but there was great joy. We sang along to John Denver, James Taylor, the Kingston Trio…and by the end of the trip, our kids knew every word.

We saw the Grand Canyon and Old Faithful, and followed the Oregon Trail. We learned and laughed and loved—and argued, of course, and had timeouts and laughed and loved again.

I'll never forget doing two loads of laundry at every KOA campsite and ending every night with s'mores by the campfire.

Many years and adventures have passed since then.

We just returned from taking 11 of our family to Disneyland. After having seven boys in a row between our two girls, we now have five granddaughters. Disneyland with five little princesses is its own adventure—very different than seven little boys trying to hang onto the double stroller.

And every time, as the little ones climbed onto the rides, there was Jack, once again with the biggest grin of all.

Adventures are so important that we are now committed that, instead of Christmas gifts each year, we will continue to do family adventures. Experiences mean so much more than "stuff."

For sure, the fathering adventure is not for the faint of heart and it takes grit! But believe me, there is a ton of glory and fun and lots of grins ahead!

~Angela Connelly

2

TOM HUCKINS

Tom Huckins grew up as the oldest of 12 siblings in rural Northern California—born in the 60s, grew up in the 70s, was in seminary, studying and working, in the US, Spain, and Italy during the 80s and half of the 90s. He met the love of his life, Lisa, after leaving the seminary; they have been married 25 years with six children, two of whom graduated from and three who are currently attending Thomas Aquinas College. Tom has been a school principal, worked at a national Catholic radio network, and now does advancement for the Augustine Institute. He and Lisa live at Rancheria Isabella, which they run with their youngest son, Thomas (12), who does a lot of the work around the ranch now and is a very skilled "outdoorsman cowboy."

Flee to the Fields

By the grace and providence of God, we were blessed to purchase a seven-acre property with a wild, untamed yard of beautiful Japanese flowers; the bulk of the land was overtaken by blackberries and wild willow. Located in the Northern California town where Lisa and I grew up,

our little town was a welcoming oasis after a six-year stint in suburban South Florida. Our parents lived in this town, as well as most of the 30-plus aunts and uncles and the 70-something cousins.

We had a few criteria as we looked: at least two acres, plentiful irrigation water, arable land, low enough elevation to grow

citrus, and, if possible, a view. God was so good to bless us with all we asked for in our little Rancheria Isabella, named for our little saint who lived for just 42 days, but who we know intercedes for our whole family.

We didn't know it fully at first, but as we developed the land, we realized it was entrusted to us for the formation of our family. We had to clear 30 years' growth of blackberries and willows, fence and cross-fence the property, set up the irrigation, plant an orchard, develop pastures, build pig pens, build chicken coops, build rabbit hutches, put in a milking barn, and of course, purchase and start breeding animals. At one point, we had 25 hogs, 13

cows, 750 meat chickens, a herd of sheep, and several dogs! Yes, it was crazy, but we later realized the ranch was a tremendous school of character and family formation.

Did the kids complain? Of course, but they also made the most beautiful observations about the joys of hard work, the pride they felt when they could handle milking a 1,000-pound Jersey cow on their own, the skills they developed in animal husbandry (a natural way to learn about the birds and the bees), repairing pipes, operating a tractor, and the ability to do good old hard work—not to mention the delicious and healthy experience of eating, cooking, and preserving the produce they had raised with their own hands. We also taught the basics of running a home-based business. This all tied in nicely with homeschooling, and it was really the place where I, as a father, could lead in unison with my wife, Lisa.

Three of our six children are currently in college, and only one is still at home full time with us. But no matter how far life has taken them from their childhood home, they all love to come home to the "ranch." Our hope is that we can keep this property as a patrimony to pass along to them. How that will work out is still a mystery, but we trust in the Father's loving providence. After all, He created man and woman to live, thrive, and multiply in love in a garden!

"Everything can be taken from a man but one thing: the last of the human freedoms—to choose one's attitude in any given set of circumstances."

– Viktor Frankl

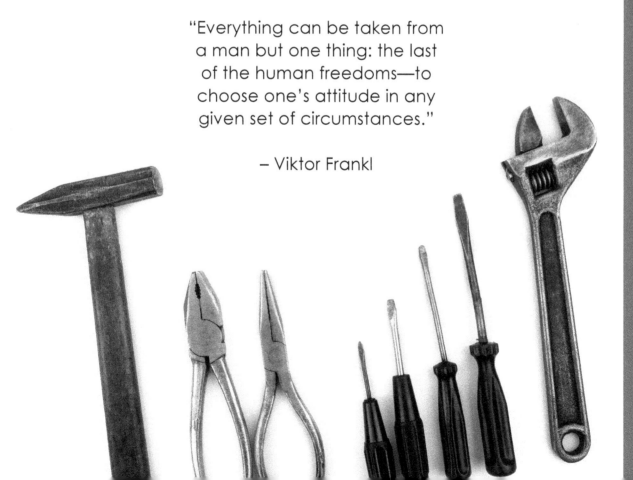

3

STEVEN MCKANNA

Steve McKanna has been married to his wife Christine for 20 years. He has been a father for over 17 years, and has five children. Steve has been a loan officer and a sales manager for 20 years and currently works for 1530 Mortgage, helping to promote green building strategies. He lives in Des Moines, Washington and enjoys the outdoors, especially boating, camping, and hiking.

I met my wife 20 years ago. I was not raised Catholic, but when I found out that she was, I quickly read a children's Bible to learn the basics and impress her. She encouraged me to become Catholic myself, but I wanted to research other religions to ensure Catholicism was right for me.

As years passed, our oldest son grew, and we had more children. I realized that my wife and I would have to be on the same page in terms of our values and ways to teach our children. So, although I had attended Mass with her, it was not until nine years into our marriage that I participated in the Rite of Christian Initiation of Adults and officially became Catholic myself.

Becoming Catholic was indeed right for me, and it has impacted the way I parent. Every day, I make a conscious choice to be involved in the lives of our children. My wife and I instill faith in their hearts in all teachable moments. I coach them in sports, listen actively, and engage in meaningful conversations even on the most hectic days. My wife and I believe in making the most of every day. We have even been blessed to travel as a family in many parts of the world to see the beauty of God's creation. We believe creating bonds with our children will result in effective teaching and disciplining.

Our goal is to raise our children with problem-solving skills so they can empathize with others. We teach them to understand emotions and respond to actions that are in line with Christ's teachings. As their father, observing my children's situations helps me to be careful not to react too quickly. Studying their thought processes and understanding the root cause of their behaviors shows me where there may be underlying fear or insecurity. I work to develop their abilities to understand others, encouraging them to find solutions and guiding their moral thought processes. I believe in guidance versus criticism. The uniqueness of their personalities means I am constantly learning and understanding the most effective way of teaching them.

Being a father is an honorable privilege from our heavenly Father. He has put me here to love and protect my children, and so I raise them to know, love, and serve *Him.* Constant prayers strengthen me to know I must ultimately trust God with the lives of our children. We feel strengthened with the help of our faithful schools and our community. My wife and I can only hope our children's choices will always reflect these beliefs and teachings we continue to instill in their hearts. Fatherhood, a great purpose here on Earth, is truly a gift from the Lord.

STEVE WESCOTT

Steve Wescott is a retired Boeing Finance executive and has been married to his wife Janey for 40 years. They have four children and 12 grandchildren. Steve is passionate about his faith, baseball, cars, and the Lord.

Memories That Last

When my dad passed away in 2013, I reflected on the many wonderful memories we shared. Although he worked long hours, he always prioritized his time with me and found ways to make it special. I wanted to have those same kinds of memories with my four sons. I too had a busy career, but I made every effort to spend time with them during their childhood. Since baseball was something we all loved, coaching their teams was among the most memorable.

As the boys grew older and busier, time together became increasingly more difficult. I realized I had to become more

intentional about creating lasting memories. We did multi-day, long-distance bike rides and fun runs. We went to auto races in Monterey and Monaco, a bowl game in San Diego, and other exciting events. But none of these compared to our epic road trip to see some of the historic baseball fields and artifacts of yesteryear.

In 2015, we visited five baseball parks in seven days, including the two oldest parks in professional baseball. We flew to Chicago, where we saw a Cubs game at the legendary Wrigley Field. From there, we rented a camper and drove through the night to spend a very special day viewing baseball's most prized possessions at the

Baseball Hall of Fame at Cooperstown. We played catch near the historic Double-day Field. Finally, we arrived in Boston to watch the perennial adversaries, the Red Sox and the Yankees, play at Fenway Park.

The memories over these seven days are profound. We were immersed in a game we all played and loved and were mesmerized by its history. We couldn't help but have flashbacks of the many baseball games we shared at local schoolyards. Spending this time with them was a dream come true, but I was reminded after our next adventure just how precious these trips would be.

In 2018, my second-oldest son organized a trip with one of his brothers and me to ride Harley Davidson motorcycles from Las Vegas through the beautiful Red Rock Canyon and the Valley of Fire. It was an extraordinary journey made even more memorable by finishing our trip in Arizona watching

spring training baseball. Every day captivated us, drawing us closer together.

Two months later, the son who organized the trip developed pneumonia and within days unexpectedly passed away. Our family was devastated, and I continue to struggle with the loss. By God's grace, I can hold on to the wonderful memories we shared together. What a blessing it was to have just completed that breathtaking trip he planned!

My hope is that my sons will continue building lasting memories with their children, a tradition started with my father. As I get older, I feel a greater sense of urgency to find that next special experience. We never know when we may have just spent our last adventure together.

JAVIER GAMEZ

Javier Gamez is an entrepreneur who was born and raised in Guatemala City. At a very young age, he proclaimed himself as an expert bike rider and appliance-and-toy-dismantler (which is probably why he ended up getting a BS in Electrical Engineering from Marquette University in 1990). Javier is also a guitar player and music lover/composer who is still dreaming about opening for Van Halen. Above all, he is an extremely grateful and happy husband and proud father of two amazing girls, and is enjoying life one day at a time!

A few days ago, a good friend of mine asked me if I could write this short essay on fatherhood. I thought to myself, *This should be easy. I mean, I've been a father for the last 25 years, and both of my daughters seem to have turned out okay, so it should be pretty straightforward to write about what it has been like.*

Boy, was I wrong! I've rewritten my ideas quite a few times and still can't truly convey what this experience has been like. I've come to realize this 24/7 job of being a father turns out to require a lot to get it right. And still, after trying to get it right, chances are you still could have done it better. But at least, you want to be able to say when they leave your house: "Dear God, I truly gave it my all bringing up this kid, and I tried to help her become the best version of herself in order to leave a positive mark in the world."

Being a father has been quite an adventure, to say the least. In my case, this adventure has been a continuous learning experience, especially for someone coming from a home with four brothers and no sisters. Having two daughters was a lesson in adapting to changes.

For example, I learned that for a young girl, a pair of shiny, plastic, LED-lit princess shoes—or as they called them, "party shoes"—were absolutely amazing. So amazing, in fact, that they felt they should always be worn, including at night, tucked in their beds. And the louder the party shoes hit the floor while walking, the cooler they were.

I also learned to host amazing tea parties in such tiny chairs; the true challenge was sitting on one without breaking it. And I learned that when it came to nail polish, pink was my color.

As they grew, being a father also helped me to learn again about algebra and arithmetic, which was a challenge even though I'm an electrical engineer.

Then, there was riding a bike. Boy, oh boy, this stage was as rewarding as it was dangerous—not for them, but for this out-of-shape dad. Again, I learned I needed to watch what I ate and hit the gym.

I learned to invent the most amazing stories to help them go to sleep and then to stealthily crawl out of bed with skills that would have won an Olympic gold medal in gymnastics, only to step on the wrong floor tile and immediately wake them up, which would force me to go back and start the whole process all over again…which, I must admit, always put a smile on my face.

A young guy who has no kids might think: *Hey, man, piece of cake, I definitely can do all of that. It actually sounds like a lot of fun!* Well, yes, fatherhood is an amazing, fun, rewarding, and incredible experience. But actually there's a lot more that truly defines the role of a father.

Unfortunately, being a father will have some very tough times as well, because as kids grow, life will start teaching them lessons. Some of those will hit them hard and bring them down, so one needs to be there to help them understand each setback that just happened and why it happened, so that next time, they will be more prepared to face it.

From the very beginning, I realized being a father required constant learning and never taking anything for granted. I tried to always be there for my kids, in the good times and especially the bad times. I tried to be by their side, listening, watching over them, noticing both the obvious and the small details.

My wife and I tried to have a very open, non-judgmental environment in our home so that our daughters felt free to talk to us, and I've always loved talking with them—yep, even during that stage of their lives where they thought they knew it all. I found that even when I thought they weren't listening, they were tuned in and taking mental notes of what we said. So, I learned the importance of being coherent with the things I said and did.

I also learned that, at times, I needed to stop talking and rather start listening to them. This meant not only hearing what

"'For I know the plans I have for you,' declares the Lord, 'plans to prosper you and not to harm you, plans to give you hope and a future.'"

– Jeremiah 29:11

they said, but also listening to what they were *not* saying, because in those unsaid words were hiding their deepest fears, sadnesses, worries and concerns, and that was where the important conversations started.

I had to learn to differentiate those times I needed to stop them before they made a mistake and those painful times I needed to allow them to mess up so they could understand about life and, as a result, grow.

So yes, being a father takes a lot of courage and commitment, but it has been the most rewarding experience in my life. It gives meaning and purpose to life and a reason to continue giving my best to everything I do. And now, with our oldest daughter married, I will start a new journey learning how to become a grandfather, in which I'm guessing my top priority will be to spoil them with tons of sugar and watch my daughter struggle putting them to sleep…but that's the way the story goes, I guess.

6

TED BAER

Ted Baer, AKA "the world's only Ranger Scout troop leader," is a Pacific Northwest native and, like his daughter, enjoys the abundance of nature the area is blessed with. He has practiced dentistry for many years, and after selling his private practice entered into his role teaching dental residents and as a part-time associate in a private practice. His greatest joy is his family—all "scouts" of one sort or another—including his beloved wife, Anne.

The World's Only Ranger Scout

I am the father of three: son, daughter, son, in that order. My wife and I are now successful empty nesters.

When our boys were younger, we were looking for ways for them to bond with other boys. This led us to the Boy Scouts, which turned out to be a positive experience as a lot of the activities included the whole family. There was one problem: Caroline, my daughter, wanted to be a Boy Scout, too.

We told her that since "boy" was in the name, she couldn't be a Boy Scout, but there was an alternative called the Girl Scouts. Caroline rejected this option, and so we arrived at a solution: we would make our own. And hence, "Ranger Scouts" was born. Caroline was the world's only Ranger Scout, and I was the world's only Ranger Scout troop leader.

We did some activities in tandem with our sons' Boy Scout troop and other things separately. She had her own sash, to which we affixed the various merit badges we managed to procure through our local Boy Scout central office store. (They were very understanding.)

The pinnacle of Boy Scouts is attaining your Eagle Scout badge, which comes with a ceremony honoring the occasion. In Ranger Scouts, the pinnacle is getting your "Owl" merit badge (because we found a large owl badge).

Prior to Caroline earning her Owl, the two of us set out on a long backpacking trip through the Olympics. On a large, flat boulder jutting out into a rushing stream, she and I wrote the Ranger Scout anthem, sung to the tune of "You're a Grand Old Flag":
We are faithful, honest, loyal, and true,
We will never abandon a friend,
In the high country, that's where we'll be,
On trails with switchbacks and bends.
We protect the meek and defend the weak,
And our courage will never end,
We are Ranger Scouts and without a doubt,
We will love Mother Earth till the end.

When Caroline earned her Owl, we had a ceremony along the Elwha River, deep in Olympic National Park, on a week-long backpacking trip with a dozen or so friends. We planned it ahead of time, and my daughter had no knowledge it was going to happen.

It was magical. I get tears just thinking about that special moment, and what it meant to her, me, and our family.

"It is a wise father that knows his own child."

- William Shakespeare

7

ALEJANDRO BOTRÁN DIAZ

Alejandro Botrán Díaz is an entrepreneur and business consultant for various startup companies ranging from television to hotels. He is a father of three and lives in Guatemala, where he was born and raised.

There is nothing like a family reunion! After many years of our kids being away for college, work, and travel, the table is crowded again, and our hearts are filled with the love and warmth of a complete family. Now, my role as a father comes into play, but in this new era, I have new tasks and a new job description: to resynchronize the family. This is fatherhood!

We've been through Pampers, toddlers, soccer games, party pickups, and most recently, empty nesting and waiting to be grandparents. All types of jobs under the single title of "fatherhood."

In this new era, "reunited" happens only briefly. Sometimes we come togeth-er at home or on family trips, but those days feel like seconds. In those precious seconds, there is a special moment where everything makes sense, where I feel fatherhood pays back the most: at the crowded table. My hope is always that the table is in harmony, in communion, and in peace. Without interruptions, without cellphones, PlayStations, TVs, or remote jobs! It's almost impossible, but that is the dream!

We are traveling through the Spanish Riviera in a black Mercedes minivan. It's the first time we are together as adults after several years, several storms, and several changes. My first mission is to create a "crowded table" on wheels in the minivan, a space where we are physically together, with room for stories, jokes, music, and laughter. I've come to find that whenever we reunite, it takes time to start vibrating at the same frequency. The frequency of the "crowded table" does not come easily: it requires work on our part as parents.

When I picture my childhood "crowded table," I see this: It's the seventies. There's a yellow pantry connected to the kitchen, a round table with many chairs, five kids, two parents, several cousins, and a baby girl in a kid's chair. The table has a Formica top and three supporting legs—who the hell designed that? If you leaned on the table with your elbows (like all our mothers told us not to), it would tumble, and Fruit Loops, Corn Flakes, and Nestum would fly all over!

Everyone is in pajamas; the younger kids have pajamas with little shoes incorporated into them. And they make noise! Kids with their hair wet, water droplets dripping down their ears, and sunburned cheeks after a long day of rigorous play. There's a dangerous combination of hungry kids and a busy mom supervising the dinner like generals, using a wooden spoon as a revolver. The kids' job is to tease the patience of the mother, and her job is not to give in. When tension is at its peak, Dad comes home from work.

"*Papa!*" All the kids radiate happiness, and he is greeted with hugs. There's a lot of energy in the room, but everyone is vibrating at a different frequency. The kids push the mother's patience to the limit, and with one loud call for order and obedience from Dad, the room's frenetic energies dial down and start

to align. With both parents sitting at the table now, the magical moment comes: the table is officially crowded.

My wife and I cherish this moment deeply. Fatherhood in the era of the empty nest is hard. Looking back to my early fatherhood days, it seemed so simple. I remember the smell of baby powder and feeling their breaths when I put them to sleep—but of course, never without first telling a story. The story was completely made up, using family characters like Aunt Angie, her cat, and her house, and maybe a train coming to town with all the animals, which escaped and wreaked havoc! My daughter asked me for the same story every night, but with a different outcome. This was where my creativity—and drowsiness—started to work.

"Dad, Dad, don't fall asleep, you are snoring!" she would plead.

"No, no, no, it's part of the story!"

Fatherhood and motherhood … as San José María said, work and family are jobs that sanctify us! Surely, those moments before we're vibrating at the same frequency around the crowded table, the moments we haven't a single ounce of patience left, are the ultimate tests, the "sanctification moments."

So, we are in the Spanish Riviera in our black Mercedes minivan, and I put on a song I dedicate to my family. The song starts, and within two claps, I'm in perfect sync with the song's claps. Everyone is looking at me weird. The song is called "The Privilege of Love" from the album *Always Friends* by the Mijares Family, a family of Mexican musicians. The parents divorced many years ago, but with their kids now grown up, they took the initiative to reunite the family and sing—a beautiful story!

A couple of days into the trip, one of my sons is driving the minivan and asks me, "Dad, what is the name of the song you played the other day?"

"'The Privilege of Love'! Why?"

And suddenly, I hear two claps, and *voilà*, he puts on the song! Fatherhood—*carajo*: it's magic, fatherhood at its best! I'm in the zone; we are in the zone, vibrating at the same frequency! All the work, all the tears, all the effort, all the anguish, all the sacrifices of fatherhood suddenly make sense!

It is the magic moment, the "crowded table moment," where it all seems worth it. It only takes a few minutes of that for everything to make sense, for the smell of baby powder, the wet hair, the Formica table, and the Fruit Loops to come back… *La zona! La zona!* The zone!

8

GEORGE SCHEUTZ

George Scheutz, the oldest of five children, grew up in Syracuse, New York. He and his wife Joyce, of 51 years, have raised their two sons in Washington State. George has worked in many capacities throughout his life: newspaper carrier, bank employee, medical technician, Marine mechanic, computer technician, ComputerLand franchise owner, Vietnam vet, and most recently at H&R Block as an Enrolled Agent for the last 20 years. Fun fact about George: his home is the brightest and best-lit home in the city during the holidays!

The Adventure of Fatherhood

When Joyce, my wife, was pregnant with our first child, we decided to name him Sam, after my college roommate, a very calm and quiet person. When our baby Sam was born, he was neither calm nor quiet! As he grew, it seemed his nightly challenge was escaping his crib and heading for our bedroom no matter what we did to prevent it.

Sam's antics grew as he did. One day while walking on top of the fence, he fell and broke his arm. So we thought sports might be a good outlet, but his small stint in baseball ended because his creativity and energy needed more freedom.

Sam got older and wanted a Nintendo game unit. Dad said, "NO!" with the caveat, "If you want one, you have to earn the money and buy the game yourself." Little did I know Sam would manage to get a paper route to start earning money. The paper route was a short distance from our home, so we allowed him to work the route. The newspaper customers loved him as he was reliable and got their paper delivered on time. Eventually he traded the smaller route for a larger one and even recruited his mom and me into his scheme. Our job was on Sundays, when the paper and inserts were huge.

As a dad, you never know the adventures your child will lead you on.

From being a paper boy, Sam graduated to being a busser at a local restaurant. His income grew and soon he was driving.

By age 18, he had purchased more vehicles than his parents ever did.

While he seemed to succeed at any business venture he tried, school was a struggle. As a father, my role continued as my wife and I supported him through his studies. Sam is now happily married and lives nearby.

As fathers, the adventure never really ends. Our hearts have joy when our kids succeed and our hearts break when they struggle. My adventure of fatherhood is the privilege of walking through it all by his side, together: father and son.

"My father gave me the greatest gift anyone could give another person, he believed in me."

- Jim Valvano

9

JACK CONNELLY

Jack Connelly is a lawyer , swimmer , golfer, and avid reader. He was a 38-year-old bachelor when he married his wife, Angela. They now have nine children and five granddaughters. Someday he will have quiet time to read again.

Hey, I'm a Dad!

I had just returned from a sabbatical in Galway, Ireland, followed by a kayak trip 1,200 miles down the Yukon. I was a partner in a large Seattle-Tacoma law firm and a carefree, swinging bachelor with a corner office…

…until the fateful day I was introduced to a woman teaching the young adult program at St. Patrick's Church. She had two children aged three and five, whose young father had died of cancer. I was hesitant but eventually attended the class. At our first meeting, she told me she wanted seven kids. *What could that mean—seven total, or seven MORE?*

A little over a year later, we were married and I had two adopted kids. A "honeymoon" baby, John Francis, soon followed. I

figured the dad thing couldn't be too tough. I had had a close relationship with my father, and he made it look easy.

But there were lessons to learn. For instance, five-year-old girls don't like being shot with a squirt gun in the bathtub. When my new son used the hose to fill the Jeep with water, I realized four-year-olds want to help but don't automatically know you wash the *outside* of a car. At our first Cub Scout campout, I watched as the other dads set up large tents, and I then pulled out the three-foot tent Angela had bought from the Target toy section. It felt a little odd spending the night with my legs sticking three feet out, but I saw that Joseph didn't notice and didn't care (and that the other dads could eventually contain their laughter). That Christmas at

4:00 a.m., I was putting together a new bicycle for Catherine, growing more and more frustrated as the hours passed. The front wheel would not spin without rubbing. I finally decided it was the first impression that mattered. I also learned that premade bikes were best.

At age 38, I had been single. At age 39, I had three children, and Angela soon became pregnant with our fourth, James. Thomas quickly followed, then Justin, Peter, and Luke. Why couldn't I make a girl? Angela's friends started giving me fairly explicit instructions on making a girl. *Really?* I thought.

Our ninth child arrived 13 years after we were married. That child, Veronica, now makes fun of me and likes to point out I was 51 when she arrived and will be 71 when she is 20. I patiently explain to her that 70 is the new 30 and I have the body of a 19-year-old.

I sincerely believe fatherhood is the best part of life. As I approach "empty nester-hood," it is hard to envision life without a little kid to wrestle. I have been blessed with 28 years of amazing family life. It has flown by. I understand now that life is full in the little things. John Lennon once said that life is what happens while you're busy making other plans.

The beauty of family life for me was found in the morning when John Francis stood up in his crib at 5:00 a.m., calling, "*Da!*" It was found in the impromptu wrestling matches when the tornado of boys invaded, running in and jumping on the bed. It was found in watching the

pride of our Irish Catholic boy who pointed at us in the stands each time he made a basket. It was found in the angst of teaching children to ride a bike and watching them fall and get up again (except Justin, who taught himself to ride). And, it was found at dinnertimes, where I envisioned having intelligent, worldly conversations like the Kennedys but couldn't get my guys to stop talking, yelling, laughing, and fighting long enough to introduce a subject. I loved the long, tumultuous, crazy, noisy, and delightful road trips, because I watched and learned who my kids were. William Channing wrote that true love is the parent of humility. In becoming a father, the greatest lesson I learned was humility—and it truly grows as I age.

Each child introduced us to a new world—new friends, new parents, new talents—none of them even close to being the same. As they grew, life filled with sporting events, school events, and scouts. Initially, it was T-ball, den meetings, soccer, back-to-school nights, and summer swim team. Over time, it turned into cross country, national crew championships, high school football and basketball, lacrosse, wrestling, and six Eagle Scouts. Then colleges, jobs, and professions. Now,

> "Who among you is wise and understanding? Let him show his works by a good life in the humility that comes from wisdom."
> – James 3:13

it is turning into marriages and a new set of little tornados in our lives.

It all feels so wonderful, though we have had our share of heartache as well. During those years, we had many hospital trips, stitches, broken bones, and surgeries. We have dealt with heartache, disappointment, drugs, addiction, car accidents, sports injuries, and more. Through it all I can say quite honestly that I never knew what I was doing. I learned to rely on faith and respond thoughtfully.

As a dad who has thoroughly enjoyed watching nine kids grow into adulthood, here are 10 thoughts:

1. Enjoy the ride. It really does go fast—very fast.
2. Pray often to your guardian angel. Pray to St. Joseph. Pray to your kids' guardian angels. Padre Pio says your guardian angels want to help you. I think a couple of our kids are on their third or fourth lives, thanks to their guardian angels.
3. Listen and care. Listen and care. Listen and care.
4. Try to never criticize out of anger. It's amazing how a father's words create or diminish a child's self-esteem. It is said that your voice becomes their inner voice.
5. Don't let your career take priority. Listen periodically to Harry Chapin's song, "Cat's in the Cradle." It's true. (Though sometimes you have to keep the car keys.)
6. Don't think you need to know the answers because you generally don't. And the kids know when you don't.
7. Your faith is everything. It's what matters most. Ultimately, each child must develop their own faith, will be called by God, and choose their answer. Be there to help. You cannot force another's faith. This is a hard lesson. Sometimes, the hardest thing to learn is that you must let go.
8. Watch their friends. Know what they are doing. Keep them busy.
9. Give all your wisdom to your child but understand that they will pay more attention to what you do than what you say.
10. Above all … love them.

SEAN MAGENNIS

Sean Magennis is the chairman of a private, multi-faceted financial services firm, Mutual Capital Alliance. He is a seasoned international business executive specializing in scaling professional services firms. He is also the national chairman of the Young Catholic Professionals, YCP. Sean's personal goals are to leverage what he continues to learn, in service of people achieving their faith, family, friendship, and work goals. When Sean is not working, he and his wife and daughter enjoy traveling, meeting new friends, exploring museums and interesting places, and sampling unique restaurants.

Fatherhood is a journey that is both unique and universal, with each experience being shaped by individual circumstances and influences. My experience of fatherhood has been shaped by many factors, but one memory stands out to me as a reflection of the chaos, adventure, fun, joy, faith, and gratitude this role entails.

As the room parent for my daughter Sofia's third-grade class at her Montessori school, I had the freedom to take time off during the week to dedicate myself to

helping. My job was to look after the garden, help the kids do planting and cleanup, and support the class projects. I loved it! I could just be a goofy dad and a friend. I could get muddy and wet and not care who saw me. I was able to observe a slice of my daughter's life that few parents were able to see. I gained an appreciation for how important teachers are; I witnessed genuine love and affection shown to the children in the teacher's care. I was humbled by the awe each child exhibited in the simple act of pulling out a weed, watching a tomato plant bear fruit, or seeing a seasonal tulip appear.

Being a room parent for my daughter's class allowed me to see the world through her eyes, to witness her joy and wonder as she discovered new things, and to appreciate the hard work and dedication of the teachers who were shaping her education. It also gave me a sense of purpose and fulfillment to be able to contribute to her school community in a meaningful way.

Fatherhood is a journey filled with both hard and holy dimensions, a role that requires us to be present and engaged in our children's lives, taking the time to appreciate the little things that often go unnoticed and valuing the relationships that shape our children. Being a room parent showed me being a father is not just about providing for our children's physical needs, but also about nurturing their emotional and social well-being. As fathers, it is our responsibility to create a safe and supportive environment where our children can thrive and grow. This way, we can create a legacy that will last a lifetime.

If you are a dad, volunteer to be a room parent. You may just learn a thing or two…

"Once we deeply trust that we ourselves are precious in God's eyes, we are able to recognize the preciousness of others and their unique places in God's heart."

– Henri Nouwen

PART 2

The Tip of the Spear

"We are born to love, we live to love
and we will die to love still more."

– St. Joseph Cafasso

The desire to protect is hardwired into the DNA of a man. More than a social construct, this is God's design of provider, guardian, and leader. From the time a little boy plays make believe or chooses his own bedtime story, you will witness good guys versus bad guys, heroes fighting for justice against the evil villains, knights of the round table, soldiers leading the charge, trees and mountains to summit, and challenges to be overcome. Nobility and strength, the call to give oneself and face fears, to fight and do what's right— these virtues are all being practiced and rehearsed in every backyard, park, and vacant lot.

Over time…

…there seems to be a built-in assumption that it all depends on *you*. An inevitable temptation to self-reliance and an invitation to a lie that humility and vulnerability are bad words. This lie is reinforced in nearly every corner of our world and in almost every conversation. Before nearly any other question or attempt to know how a man is made, the question is asked…"And what do you *do*?"

This question includes an innate assumption that what a man "does" is tantamount to what his worth is. And, in this day and age, what his worth is, often has to do with the money he makes and the stuff he possesses. However, ask any man about his value, and the deepest longing of his heart and if he has ever had or taken time to reflect—and the inquirer is sincere—there come answers of a much different kind. You will hear about legacy, family, hopes, and dreams that place an occupation in its right (proper) order—i.e., a catalyst, a means to an end.

"Courage" is a heart word. The root of the word courage is cor—the Latin word for heart. Over time, this definition has changed and today we typically associate courage with heroic and brave deeds. A man called to be courageous is ultimately called to a life of love, and loving with one's whole heart. This is not merely a wimpy, romantic love depicted with poems and flowers; the love that real men are called to, from the beginning of time, is selfless, sacrificial love, akin to the love that bore the torture of the world and ultimately the spear, to save His beloved.

This love poured out to the last drop is the type of love we all long for and that we are dying to find and receive. The love that wills the good of the other, even if it means laying down our own life; this is the courageous love that leads the life of a heroic man. And this love is not cheap… in fact, it costs everything. It costs the toil of the brow, as Genesis refers to. It looks different in every home and heart and yet it bears the same heavy and holy privilege

of doing whatever it takes to provide and protect the ones that have been entrusted to its care.

The temptation to self-reliance finds its roots in the fact that increasingly we are instructed "every man for himself," "eat or be eaten," "only the strongest survive" (or worse, only the strongest, *should* survive), "pull yourselves up by your bootstraps," and so on.

Friedrich Nietzche wrote, "He who has a why to live for can bear almost any how." The *why* can look different for each person (and ought to) and yet what love requires you to bear is truly the cost of this life, of one's whole life, of one's only life.

"We are hard pressed on every side, but not crushed; perplexed, but not in despair; persecuted, but not abandoned; struck down, but not destroyed.
We always carry around in our body the death of Jesus, so that the life of Jesus may also be revealed in our body."

- 2 Corinthians 4:8-10

~Megan McDaniel

11

BOB TURNER

Bob Turner has been married to Christine for 32 years, raising a family of seven children. He grew up in Tacoma, Washington and was a 1983 graduate of West Point. After serving in the army and earning an MBA, he became an associate partner with the global consulting firm Accenture. He devoted seven years in co-founding Gloria's Angels, a nonprofit service agency for families battling cancer; currently he works as a program manager for Microsoft and volunteers as a youth minister. In his spare time, over the last 34 years, he has officiated high school wrestling.

Insights from a Large Family

It seemed like the perfect choice for a New Year's Eve family game–Apples to Apples. For those unfamiliar with that game, it would take too much of this essay to explain the rules. But, trust me, this game requires no skill from the players whatsoever. Everyone in our large family could play, from Mom and Dad to our seven kids, who range in age from five up to 19 years old.

Ah, time to create some new, joyful memories to add to our holiday scrapbook of life. (Quick, call Norman Rockwell and tell him to bring the canvas and oils.) Well, first came a few crying fits from the youngest ones. Then came teens frustrated by the random nature of a game that allowed their 11-year-old brother to win so quickly. So it was time to move onto something else. (My apologies to Norman Rockwell for wasting his time.)

We did not originally intend to have seven children. Back when we had only one baby, it took more than one bi-weekly paycheck to cover the mortgage. We never considered having a life with more than two or three kids. And it was hard to imagine how you could love subsequent children as much as your first one. We never envisioned having at least one child in diapers for 17 STRAIGHT YEARS either. But then again, we never chose to have a family based on the cold calculus of checkbook balances or some undefined limita-

tion of our capacity to love. Similar to the analogy of the frog remaining in the tepid water, heating up toward the boiling point, we didn't jump right into having seven children—we got there one step at a time. Each child came from a strong faith affirmed by ever-expanding measures of love.

Large families are rare nowadays in America. The diverse tapestry of our society benefits from having a broad range of family structures. I believe our large family can provide a needed boost of happiness in a world that often struggles with grim realities such as economic recessions, terrorism, and natural disasters. My kids participate in a piano recital at a retirement home each Christmas season. Each

year, I see lots of smiles from the residents that watch the performance, then, later, interact with our children. Or maybe they are reassured to know that seven more people will enter the workforce to pay into the Social Security fund. Either way, it's heartening to see those smiles.

Granted, life for our family has challenges too. The older kids groaned at Disneyland when it came time to leave and they wanted to spend a few more hours in the park. Unfortunately, the youngest ones were melting down and needed to go back to the hotel room. Since we only had one vehicle, we all had to leave. (At least the line got nine people shorter on Space Mountain for everyone else.)

There was also the time I had to bring two little boys to the restroom at a restaurant. I struggled helping one wash his hands while the other, unexpectedly, behind my back, decided to sit on the urinal and do what one ought to only do on a toilet–well, those are dilemmas I don't wish upon anyone. But, in fairness, the joys overwhelm the hardships daily. Even though my oldest is away at college, I have the privilege of being greeted daily by the beauty and innocence of hugs delivered by little ones who still assign names and personalities to their stuffed animals. Their

love keeps me young.

So, yes, I see people roll their eyes when our crew shows up at a restaurant. Hopefully you will feel rewarded when your party of two gets seated 30 minutes before a table opens up large enough for us. Or maybe you will appreciate it when my oldest son holds the door open for you as you enter. And perhaps you will chuckle when you hear our five-year-old tell her grandma, "The reason I like you is not 'cause you're fat, but because you have a nice face."

If not, enjoy a laugh at my expense as you see me heading toward the bathroom with those two little boys.

"God's mercies are new every morning, not because God has some obligation to you— but as an affirmation of you."

– Ann Voscamp

12

RIZALDO SALVADOR

Rizaldo "Riz" Salvador is a colonel who has more than 20 years of leadership in the U.S. Army. He is a native of the Philippines and a first-generation American raised in Cleveland, Ohio. Currently, Colonel Salvador is the Chief of Staff in the 593rd Expeditionary Sustainment Command at Joint Base Lewis McChord, Washington. Riz has been married to his wife, Heather, for 24 years and they have 10 children.

Our Table

Heather and I decided early in our marriage to live out our faith by sharing it with our children in the most natural way we could find: coming together each day at the dinner table.

We have come to realize in these early years that eating together is like a classroom for a family, and our children are the students. As the primary teachers of our "class," we embrace our vocation as parents for the children already born and the children yet to come.

As we became open to God's plan for our family size, I knew it was a leap of faith to accept whatever number of children we received. We joked during the early years that Heather wanted four kids and I wanted six. Having 10 children, she received her four and I received my six! We did not know the future size of our class, but we knew the curriculum would have to be excellent to produce future saints.

Both Heather and I came from different cultural backgrounds, but neither of us grew up eating together as a family.

Our parents worked schedules that made us into latchkey kids who often ate frozen dinners in front of the television set. As I reflect on my childhood, I ache for the missed memories and moments. Correcting this aspect of upbringing for our children was the first and most important step to tackle.

As we received each child and moved around the world, our priority when selecting a home was always to identify the layout of the dining room, the most important room in our home. Just as we come together at Mass to share in the Eucharist, we gather around the dining room table nightly to eat together and share in the divine.

The dining room, as the main family classroom, is a 365-day-a-year encounter with our faith. It provides an encounter with God each day, and we parents share in that encounter by transmitting these gifts of faith. Sitting there makes it possible to create a daily habit that builds each child's character. Though we are far from perfect at doing it every day, we have made eating dinner together the family's most sacrosanct routine. During this routine, Heather and

"How can there be too many children?
That is like saying there are too many flowers."

– Saint Mother Teresa

I see miracles, each with the potential to impact the world now and into the future.

We begin each meal with prayer, an acknowledgment to God as the priority in our lives. We teach our children table manners: I am served last to demonstrate my role as a servant leader, and we wait for Heather to take the first bite of food before eating. The older children serve the younger ones, both as a matter of practicality and as an act of selfless service to others. We then share how the day went, going around the table giving "highlights and bummers." We sometimes play a spontaneous game of Catholic trivia.

It all plays into the vision of the table as a classroom for life. Eating together is a way for our family to grow in service and holiness together. For Heather and me, it is the most important part of our vocation as parents.

13

JASON WHALEN

Mayor Jason Whalen has served on the Lakewood, Washington City Council since 2010. Jason was commissioned as a second lieutenant through Gonzaga University's Army ROTC Program. He served in Germany, and then attended Gonzaga Law School. Jason cofounded Ledger Square Law and continues to build community in many ways. He has been married to his wife, Gael, for 35 years and they have three daughters, Olivia, Clare, and Alison.

Reflections of One Father's Voice

I am the proud "girl dad" of Olivia, Clare, and Alison Whalen. My daughters are my greatest accomplishment, my source of pride and joy, and they serve as daily reminders of the many blessings in my life.

My own parents were hardworking, Montana-born members of the Greatest Generation. They lived through the Great Depression, went to college on shoestring budgets, and, following my dad's Naval service during World War II, married and started our family.

Our family made many moves to support Dad's career. I was the new kid in school every two years until high school. As the youngest of four, I too often experienced my father as a mere provider and disciplinarian rather than a source of inspiration, wonder, and physical affection. To be sure, I knew he was proud of us and our accomplishments as we grew older, but I also knew I wanted to parent differently.

Fortunately, we "modern" dads have the opportunity to embrace fatherhood free from the rigid societal box of "manhood" that too often confined our own dads. I knew this fatherhood gig was going to be special when I participated in the birth of our first child, Olivia. To be present and involved in the birth of a child is a true gift—one I will never forget! The immediate rush of love for one's child is an incredibly powerful emotion. Four years later, Clare joined our family.

Happy with our "perfect" family of four, Gael and I proceeded to plant our roots in Lakewood, Washington, and build a three-bedroom home. Soon, we learned we would need a fourth bedroom! Alison would be joining us—a bit unexpectedly, but still welcome! Alison chose to arrive a few hours after we concluded a political event held for my first campaign in Lakewood, and she has been a part of my public service journey her entire life.

I have been blessed to be present for and participate in each of my children's births. I have watched with pride as they graduated from college and embarked on their careers. I have been honored to walk the first one down the aisle to marry my first son-in-law, surrounded by the overflowing love of family and friends. I have relished having silly times, cooking fun meals, and playing games. We laugh, we love, we hug, we cry, and we even run

together. No matter where they go and how they grow, they know I love them and will always be there for them.

The beauty of fatherhood has been the opportunity to nurture each of these young ladies on their unique paths to adulthood. The joy of fatherhood has been attending the cheerleading events, the gymnastic competitions, the crew weekends, and the myriad of cross-country tournaments, shouting until hoarse.

The blessing of fatherhood has been our ability to provide our girls an incredible life through travel, a stable home, and a village of caring friends and adults who love and support them. I am incredibly proud to have nurtured their own high standards and commitments to serve others in the pursuit of their own dreams. Fatherhood is a wonderful journey. This "girl dad" loves every minute of it.

14

JEFFREY MCVICKER

Jeffrey McVicker is the franchise owner of several Subway restaurants and a director of the Washington State Fair. He has been married for 32 years to his wife Ellen and is the father of three daughters. He has an insatiable desire to build and support communities.

A Dad of Three Daughters

"I feel sorry for you when they become teenagers!"

"Man, you're surrounded by women!"

"What did you do to deserve that?"

Being a dad to three amazing daughters, I heard these comments repeatedly as they grew up. Honestly, I am honored to have been a dad to my three girls. Having daughters has been one of the greatest joys in my life, and raising girls with my wife has been a privilege, not a burden.

Looking back, I can't claim I had it all figured out perfectly, but there are several things I've learned in the past 30 years:

- Get involved and stay involved in their lives: extracurricular activities, music, social media, careers, and beyond. Make sure they know you are always there for them and interested in what they are doing.
- Always let them know they are loved and that you will be there to support them in whatever they need. Some-

times, they need a lot: a companion while they go to traffic court, a ride to the emergency room, a truck and some muscle when they move out, and that same truck and muscle when they move back home again.

- Love your spouse. My daughters watched closely how I treated their mom. Showing love, kindness and respect to their mom was a priority. I can only hope this means something to them.

- Be their first dance partner and continue to dance through life with them. I started dancing with them early, and each of them had their special song: "Let's Go Fly a Kite," "I Could Have Danced All Night," and "You Are My Sunshine." It was a thrill to see their young faces when I would randomly ask them to dance. I went to their recitals and have hours of their dancing on videotape. The annual school father-daughter dance was a big event in our lives. They would dress up, and I would take turns asking each of them to dance at the event. My eldest daughter asked me to do a choreographed dance at her wedding. We broke out with a medley of dance moves for our

> "Fathering is not something
> perfect men do, but something
> that perfects the man."
>
> - Frank Pittman

own grown-up father-daughter dance. I hope my girls learned joy in the freedom of expressing themselves, I hope they learned how to be treated with love and respect, and I hope they had fun being silly with their dad!

- Love your children for who they are. All my girls are different in their styles, activities, and personalities. I love who each of them have become, and even though they are all on their own now, I still tell them they are beautiful, both inside and out.

- Demonstrate the qualities of a supportive, hardworking, and generous husband and father. I hope this translates into what my daughters value as qualities in their future partners.

- Take responsibility for your mistakes. There have been times when I have said and done the wrong things as a father. I have learned that apologizing goes a long way in creating a loving and constructive path forward.

- Be a memory maker. Plan family trips and outings; make special dinners. We don't know how much time we have on this earth, so create memories with your family.

I have loved being a father to my three daughters, and I have recently become a "Papa," too. I have already started dancing with our granddaughter, and I will do all I can to support her parents as they raise the next generation of our family.

"I always dreamed about being a pro quarterback but more than anything, I wanted to be like my dad."

- Tim Tebow

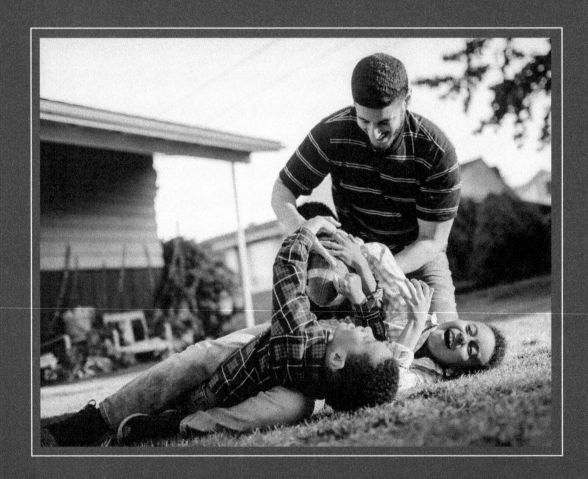

15

KEVIN PERRY

Kevin Perry was born and raised in Waterford, Connecticut, and served in the Navy for four years. He owned KM Perry Trucking, Inc. for 35 years and is currently a corporate auditor for Quality Transport, Inc. Kevin and his wife, Laura, perfected the art of paintballing as they raised their two sons. They currently reside in Gig Harbor, Washington.

I think most fathers, to some degree, go through life checking boxes, making lists, and completing tasks. Recently, it dawned on me that I could confidently check a monumentally important box: "Be sure my boys grow up to be good men."

I am the father of two boys, ages 26 and 30, and I have been privileged to experience the adventures of fatherhood. Long ago, I read that mothers raise good boys and dads raise good men. That is our challenge and our job. I became a father at age 33. I worked long hours when my boys were young and was gone a lot. This put Mom in the lead when it came to raising good boys. Over the years, along with a firm foundation of faith in God and love of family, both of our boys were exposed to music, art, science, history, languages, and sports. My wife and I believed in the philosophy of exposing them to a lot of different things and letting them follow what piqued their interest. An unexpected joy for me was when each boy gravitated

toward my two passions—Taekwondo and paintball. While I was good at both sports, my boys took them to another level.

My oldest son, Dylan, immersed himself in martial arts, training with my former master. Through hard work and dedication, he earned his first-degree black belt in Taekwondo at age 18. Dylan's belt was presented and tied in place by the man who had trained me before my son was born. The pride I felt at his accomplishment was overwhelming, and I will never forget that moment.

My younger son, Nico, loved to play paintball with me. At age 15, he was selected to be on a professional paintball team— the youngest player on one of only 12 professional teams in the world. We spent many years traveling the national circuit together until he left for college, making memories that would last a lifetime.

I cherish those years traveling to tournaments with both of my boys, immersed in their sports and hanging out with people who shared our passions. But their dedication to their sports is just a small part of who they are. I am most proud that both of my boys are deeply committed to their faith and to their family, and I know they try to live in a way that is good. They are respectful, kind, and strong. They are both unwavering in their commitment to do the right thing, even when that may bring friction among their peers. With the help of God, family, and friends, I am blessed to say my good boys truly have become good men.

16

JOHN AMUNDSEN

John Amundsen is an Army officer, finance manager, and lead detention officer with youth. John and his wife Wendy have raised their three kids in Tacoma, Washington. John enjoys swimming, the outdoors, hiking, camping, adventuring, and is a gifted dog whisperer. He strives to daily practice his faith as well as his fatherhood.

"Fatherhood." What does that word mean to me?

As a young man, I was certain I could handle any challenge on my own. When I became a father, I realized there was more to life than me. Fatherhood has been the most humbling experience of my life. When I asked God the Father for guidance, I began to see the light. It was only a glimmer at first, but I had to open my eyes and heart to see His brilliant light.

I grew up in a large Catholic family, number five of seven children. Fatherhood was always expected of me. Wendy, my wonderful wife and partner for life, is one

of three adopted children. My parents repeatedly asked me when we were having children, as opposed to Wendy's, who understood family differently.

Until 1992, Wendy and I lived in Philippsburg, Germany. I was a US Army Officer and Wendy worked for the US government. During our free time, as we rode the train to ancient castles or pedaled our bikes through the German countryside, we shared our hopes and dreams of becoming parents.

When we returned to the US, we had a brief stint in Virginia before making our new home near Fort Lewis, Washington.

We were approaching our fourth anniversary and pregnant with our first child when I received orders to deploy to Somalia. How could this happen? This was not in the plan!

In the winter of 1993, after I had departed and after Wendy had endured seven weeks of bed rest, our beautiful daughter, Nikita (Niki), arrived. Just hearing my child was born changed my whole perspective on fatherhood. I sat in Africa, praying to God for guidance on how I would become a good earthly father. I knew I had to provide, protect, guide, and love this precious new gift. Four long months later, I met my daughter at the McChord airport as a Seattle news team captured the homecoming.

After welcoming a second amazing daughter, Tatiana, I left the Army with a knee injury. Zachariah, our wonderful son, was born a couple of years later.

The responsibility and uncertainties that accompanied parenting were enormous, but those three wonderful children brought me more joy than I could have ever imagined. A trip to the park, endless games, telling Jesus's parables, and eating at Pao's Donuts soon became the highlight of my day. I brought my children to church, drove them to school, and even coached their sports teams.

Through career and health challenges, I have learned to persist even when I was knocked down—literally. In 2008, while walking the dog with Niki on a beautiful Sunday evening, I was physically assaulted a block from our home. Niki called for help as I lay unconscious on the street, and she saved my life. But our lives were forever changed. Recovering from a head injury is a long and arduous journey. Our lives were turned upside down, and the financial toll on our family was overwhelming. Without notice, my life flashed before me. I met Jesus in the ambulance as I wavered in and out of consciousness. As a victim, the control I thought I had over my life vanished.

My children's big, strong dad was now a confused and helpless man. Fatherhood took on a new appearance. I focused on regaining strength and retraining my brain as they carried on with life around me. I can only hope that when my children look back on this time, they remember my determination and persistence to never give up.

I lost my job in the finance industry due to my injury, so I made a career change and began working in juvenile detention. I now began facing youth who had committed crimes like the one in which I had been a victim. Many of the youth in detention do not have moms and dads to guide them through life's challenges with honesty and integrity. Fatherhood comes in many forms: my hope is to mentor and encourage youth to find God and purpose in life.

The attitude you have as a parent is what your kids will learn from more than what you tell them. They don't remember what you try to teach them. They remember what you are."

- Jim Henson

Now, as a father of adult children, I realize that fatherhood can mean walking next to my children, listening to them talk, and withholding my comments unless advice is requested. When I talk to God, I may not always hear an immediate reply: it is the same with us. They no longer need me to teach them a sports technique or how to solve a math problem. This is extremely challenging for me, as my friends and family will tell you I like to talk and share all my ADHD-fueled thoughts and ideas with anyone in the vicinity.

My children love each other and know how to share their love and compassion with people in this world. Knowing that God loves them even more than I do brings me incredible joy. I love Wendy and my children more each day, and I want to walk beside them as Jesus walks with me, in a state of love and compassion. If I am not leading with love, then nothing I say will matter, because I have learned the right idea with the wrong approach will not reach anyone. I am so proud of each one of my children, and I ask for their forgiveness for any wrongs or hurts that I have caused and that they be patient with me along my journey of fatherhood.

Fatherhood is a lifelong journey of discovery, leadership, and listening.

17

PHILIP JESSE

Phil Jesse lives in Tacoma, Washington, in the home his grandparents had built in 1956, with his wife Anne Marie, and tries not to helicopter parent their four gainfully employed grown children. Along the way, he has been active in supporting St. Patrick Parish and School, and Boy Scout Troop 299. He maintains his ties to alma maters Bellarmine Prep ('82), Gonzaga University ('86), and Seattle University ('91). Currently Phil leads the family business now operating in its 46th year as a specialty structural steel fabricator.

Reflections

My experience of fatherhood's ups and downs can be summarized by the words "lead," "provide," and "protect."

Remember Joseph from the Bible, who led Mary to Egypt to escape King Herod? That was a gutsy move! As fathers, it might appear easy for us to make decisions, but it's not so easy when we know deep down we'll have to own the consequences. Are you willing to lead from the front? Sometimes, a course of action needs to be taken, and people in your life will be looking to you and relying on you for that decision in the moment, whether they say so or not.

It would be too easy to list the obvious things a father should provide, like food, shelter, and financial stability. How about something else, like wisdom or counsel? Do your sons and daughters know they can come to you in a time of struggle with any problem in their life? If you get to that level, the easy part is when what you have to say is what they want to hear. It's not so great when you have to say what they *need* to hear. But you do what you do because that's the job God gave you: to provide wisdom.

A new parent may visit their newborn's bedroom every hour to check that the room temperature is just right, the baby is positioned just so, or just "to make sure." That's the protective nature of parents, and we can chuckle about those days once they've passed. People think about physical protection, like protecting a newborn from a chill. But I also think about spiritu-al protection. Are you providing spiritual protection, or are you leaving your son or daughter exposed?

I have always said the happiest day of my life was the day my first son was born. That's despite an occasional playful correction from my wife: I was a father nine months before his birth, of course. That day was 30 years ago. There have been many joyful occasions along the way, and I reflect on those with gratitude. Gratitude for what? For the gift of fatherhood. To whom? To the One who invented it.

18

DAVID LUCAS

David Lucas served more than 21 years in the United States Marine Corps with multiple combat deployments. He is the father of two teenage boys and looks forward to a long life with his wife and sons, sharing many experiences and raising honorable and faithful men.

Deployed Fatherhood

Becoming a father is a great gift from the Lord, but it brings with it one my greatest fears.

I feel the responsibility of fatherhood and what it means to raise men who will someday lead their own families and fortify society. The worry for my boys' health and their development in my absence is far greater than any fear of personal pain or injury.

As a Marine officer, I have had many deployments. During one deployment to Afghanistan, I thought it was possible I could be killed. I was afraid, not for my own well-being, but for that of my family and the future of my sons. During this deployment, I took the opportunity to write a journal for my boys. I wanted to leave something for them that would communicate my messages in case I would not be able to share them personally.

The notebook I used, a green logbook, is abundant in the military and easily obtained, even when deployed. I took one and started to capture the thoughts and experiences I wanted to share with my boys. I divided the book by age so the entries would be appropriate for their development. In addition, I included the writings of other men whom I knew could be good examples for my sons and share their expertise with them.

Since my return, the partnership with other men has become a goal for the boys' well-rounded development. I am very good at some things, but there are many gaps in my skills. So, I now try to connect my sons with honorable men who have great skills and are willing to share them with my sons in a manner that will help them develop to be honorable and faithful men themselves. My intent is that these experiences will help prepare them to lead their families and choose their own paths in life. This strategy is like the effort some parents make to get their children into a variety of sports—but

my mission is to see them through to Heaven as honorable and faithful men!

My responsibility as a father is to raise my boys to be men who will not only lead their families and raise their children faithfully, but also lead our society. This responsibility doesn't diminish in my absence. Therefore, I look at how I can best fulfill my vocation as a father and head of my family.

I encourage you, reader, to look at how you want your own children raised, and to capture those thoughts in writing. It's difficult to take time away from other activities to share the goals of your vocation as a father, but the value for your family and you is immeasurable.

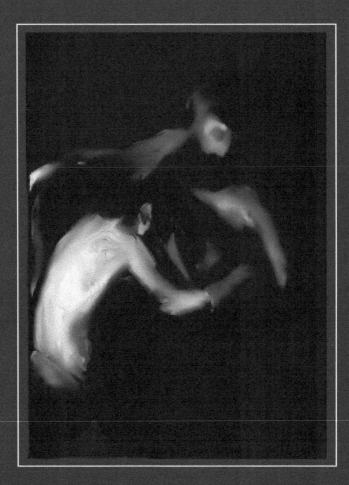

Prodigal Son by Justin Connelly

PART 3

The Hard and the Holy

The dad on the evening news looked beaten, yet something in his voice was strong. Though his eyes were swollen from crying, they somehow looked intently into all of our hearts on the other side of the camera.

His 12-year old daughter, Imaculee, had just been killed.

She and her best friend had been walking together on a side road by their homes earlier that day. A stolen, speeding commercial truck mercilessly ran the two girls over and kept going.

Before the viewers' eyes, the grieving father, was pleading with the community to help find the white, long bed truck. For days the mystery unfolded on the news updates until finally the truck and the driver were found. As it turned out, the driver had been high on drugs, had a history of grand theft, and, most heartbreakingly, was not sorry.

The grace-filled father, having just lost his precious daughter, then did something extraordinary. He again looked intently into the hearts of the viewers at home and proclaimed on the news that even though the driver was not sorry, he and his wife and family would find a way, with God's help, to forgive him.

This father led the candlelight vigil of prayer at the accident sight. The community turned out in droves, Imaculee's entire family, including her seven brothers and sisters, led the prayer.

I have never seen such grace in the midst of brokenness—such leadership, such love for a child, such trust in God, such surrender.

Beauty in the brokenness.

Yes, fatherhood embraces the hard and the holy of life.

Fatherhood is not just cheering children on for their first steps; it's not just teaching them to fish and ride bikes. It's ultimately walking them to God and to our eternal home.

In this chapter, "The Hard and the Holy," you will hear from Imaculee's father, John Goldade. You will hear real stories from other real dads who have faced other hard and holy moments. With sadness and strength, with fear and courage and in the midst of deep vulnerability, these dads share their hearts—fathering through illness, through disabilities, and through death.

You will witness the difference that grace and faith make in the hardest moments of our lives.

~Angela Connelly

Marriage is hard. Divorce is hard.
Choose your hard.
Obesity is hard. Being fit is hard.
Choose your hard.
Being in debt is hard. Being financially disciplined is hard.
Choose your hard.
Communication is hard. Not communicating is hard.
Choose your hard.
Life will never be easy. It will always be hard.
But we can choose our hard.
Choose wisely.

MICHAEL VAN HECKE

Michael Van Hecke is the founder, president, and publisher of JM Educational Group, also known as The Institute for Catholic Liberal Education, a national leader in Catholic School Renewal and the Catholic Textbook Project, a company producing the first history textbooks specifically for Catholic Schools in nearly 50 years. He has been a Catholic educator for 35 years; most recently he served as Headmaster of St. Augustine Academy in Ventura, California for 20 years. He received a B.A. in Classical Liberal Arts from Thomas Aquinas College and an M.Ed. in Educational Administration from the University of North Texas. As a consultant and speaker, Michael loves to share his passion for Catholic liberal education across the country. When not doing that, he enjoys life with his wife, doting on grandchildren and tending their avocado ranch in bucolic Santa Paula, California.

Somewhere, sometime, some wise person said, "The key to happiness is low expectations." I am happy.

I had little idea of what to expect to *get* from life, but throughout high school and college, I started to figure out what I needed to *give* in life: I wanted to live with my eyes fixed on Heaven. So, with no definitive expectations but a deepening passion to pursue an end which promised eternal happiness, I guess I set myself up pretty well.

Then life started to happen, and I found out I did have some expectations. When I married God's gift to me, Jessie, we expected we would share the same path as all our good Catholic peers who were getting married, filling a sedan, then a minivan, and ultimately a *maxi*-van as the years progressed. It was just what happened with a good Catholic marriage open to life and God's generosity.

But He had other plans: Jessie and I could not conceive.

After prayers, suffering, fear, and pain, we finally readjusted the expectation and blindly wondered what the heck God was doing. Can you imagine how perplexing and frustrating it is to see pregnancies out of wedlock, babies being born in crack houses, and worst of all, babies being aborted? The pain was searing and recurring. Yet our marriage was forged in this suffering, and our ultimate desire for Heaven was undimmed. Our expectations were recalibrated to low—or maybe we just "let go and let God." Regardless, not expecting

much of anything going forward, every gift provided much greater happiness and gratitude. We really appreciated every gift, and we still do. I am happy.

Part of that happiness has been realizing how our infertility was a blessing in disguise, because God had a beautiful plan to build our family. We adopted a beautiful little princess who was a spark of joy and love in our lives. Then God gave us a miraculous pregnancy and the most amazing baby boy, whose first two weeks were spent in the NICU receiving spinal and brain surgery. 30-some surgeries, an Eagle

Scout honor, a college graduation, and an adaptive athlete resume later, our son is a success. Not finished yet, God gave us another spark of joy through the gift of adoption. As I recall this, though, she was more than a spark: she was a lightning bolt of joy, fun, and curiosity. Our three children continue to be a deep font of happiness today.

It has been a challenging journey, one I bless the Lord for. I am glad *He* is the

Author and not I. What a beautiful life He has written for us. We will never make it as poster parents for the big Catholic family, but that is not our call—our call is to be faithful. We used to be sensitive about our family size because it seemed like in our communities, large families were the norm—after all, if you are open to life, that is the way it goes for most people. But in our lifetime of reading lives of the saints, we find that it is not having 7, 10, or 15 kids that makes you a good Catholic, but a conviction to be a saint. Many saints came from or had small families, but they lived for God. That is our baptismal call. God's story allowed us to live this call deeply and share it with thousands of others in our decades of work in Catholic schools. Our work within a few schools has now grown to include hundreds of schools across the country in more than two-thirds of the nation's dioceses. This was not something we expected or could have written—but God could.

The greatest blessing of all is that the trials and challenges brought into focus our true vocation. Our marriage thrived, and my wife really showed me the way to holiness. Our furnace forged us into the "one" we vowed to become on our blessed wedding day. This allowed us to give the best thing a parent can hope to give his child: a good marriage. God has multiplied our small gift to him. Our tidy little family of three has grown to fifteen in these last eight years with marriages and babies, and as I write these words, the tenth grandchild is on the way.

I guess God has crowded our table after all!

"The presence and involvement of a father is unlike anything else in the universe. That's because dads mimic what our heavenly Father does for us, His children—He protects, shelters, comforts and loves."

- Joe Battaglia

JOHN GOLDADE

John Goldade has been married to his wife Amber for over 22 years. He is a proud father of eight. He lives in Tacoma, Washington and has worked with people with developmental disabilities for the past 18 years.

I am blessed. God has always taken care of me. I have never had to work too hard or suffer too much. I have always been well fed (and, consequently, well rounded). It's not that I've never struggled, but God has always come through. I haven't lived a pampered life—at least not by American standards—but I've always had what I needed, and most of everything I've wanted. He has continued to bless me, even though I've turned my back on Him more times than I would like to admit.

God greatly blessed me when, out of loneliness, I walked down to the shore at Owen's Beach one sunny spring day and threw out a prayer for a wife. Not too

long after, He blessed me with a wife— and she's a marvelous one, too. From that point on, it was no longer I, but us.

He blessed us with six daughters, then a boy, and then one last daughter. My blessings had only just begun, because I discovered I loved the little bodies, the little smiles, and the clever little comments. I loved the unstoppable curiosities, the big discoveries, and the bigger cover-ups. I cherished the hugs and kisses and the silly games.

I am blessed by my teens who try on different faces, not realizing how beautiful they are. I am blessed by a boy whose mission is to jump, climb, and shout. I am blessed as I treasure the girls who are always gathering around giggling over the latest thing and giving me lessons on the latest slang. I love when they tell me they love me by teasing me for my belly, implying I'm old, and making bald jokes.

In a terrible tragedy, we lost our 12-year-old daughter in January 2022. I can't pretend it didn't hurt then and doesn't still most days. But then, and even now, I have never been mad at God for taking her away. Not even once, not even for a moment. How could I? Look how blessed I am.

My wife and I always thought it was kind of crazy, but we kept saying yes, and God kept blessing us. It's not always easy. It's certainly not affordable. It's definitely illogical … but He keeps on blessing us. Where there's His will, there's His way, and it's amazing how it always works out.

"Finally, all of you, be of one mind, sympathetic,
loving toward one another, compassionate, humble.
Do not return evil for evil, or insult for insult; but,
on the contrary, a blessing, because to this you were called,
that you might inherit a blessing."
– 1 Peter 3:8-9

PETER LEMMON

Peter Lemmon is an Of Counsel attorney (that means a gray hair amongst younger lawyers) with Lloyd-Lemmon, a law firm in Front Royal, Northern Virginia. In the law, Peter has argued small cases and handled trials, representing cities, counties, and the State of California's Secretary of State as far as the United States Supreme Court, where he prevailed with his incredible legal team. As the father of 17 (three miscarried), he is either constantly praying for, sitting down with, or on the phone with one of his children. He loves music, has written over 200 songs, and lived a year in Nashville. In his retirement, he would like to get back to music full time, but in the meanwhile, his local parish, his wife, Kari, the kids, the house, and the law firm—and his friends, extended family, and community—keep him busy, happy, and out of trouble.

I have often asked myself how I ended up around this crowded table of 17! But then again, I did grow up as the baby of seven, my parents eschewing the contraceptive mentality of their peers and having us all within nine years. I loved my big family and all my siblings and our big, crazy life and all our pets—chickens, dogs, cats, parakeets, parrots, and even a monkey!

My father was handsome and larger than life, with a big smile and an even bigger laugh and heart. I adored him and have always wanted to be like him. He presided at our family table dinner hour. Everybody could speak (one at a time), and everyone pretty much did. We were safe and happy.

I always felt close to Jesus, which was largely my mother's doing. She loved Him so much and passed that on to me. Her faith in Him was the touchstone for everything she did. They were amazingly good parents.

My own journey as a father has been a little less "normal," though it started the same as most. I attended Thomas Aquinas College, where I met and married my sweetheart, Jackie.

Her father, whom I greatly respected, was careful not to give advice after we were married. But before that, when I asked him for Jackie's hand, he said an extraordinary thing—and he prefaced it by saying he knew I was not asking for his advice but he was going to give it anyway.

He said: "Be willing to be 'hated' by your children, especially when they are teenagers, so that your wife can be a mother."

This advice was hard to grasp at first: in my own nuclear family, it was my mother who had done most of the disciplining (which we regarded as nagging), and it was my father we all adored. Nonetheless, it seemed wise to me, and its rightness has been confirmed over the years.

Therefore, I was a constant, ready, and probably stern disciplinarian. I found that my children did indeed go to their mother for comfort and mothering. And so, Jackie and I proceeded over the next 17 or so years to bring nine beautiful children into the world.

However, this was where my ordinary fatherhood ended.

About a year after the birth of our ninth child, Jackie died of Valley Fever, a soil fungus. She suffered horrific headaches and fevers spiking to 105 for more than a year, and we watched our beautiful wife and mother deteriorate before our eyes until she looked like a very old woman and passed at only 39 years old.

In the months following Jackie's passing, the rest of my world blew up around me. Within a year, it seemed everything had been stripped from me except for my children and a few close friends and family members. I suffered employment termination and lack of direction, and I wondered if it would be best to move away and attempt a new start.

Without Jackie, I became both mother and father to my children. This, of course, drastically changed how, when, and whether I disciplined. After a series of self-sacrificing nannies helped us, I moved the entire family back to Northern California where I hoped for that fresh start.

"Being a father, to our own children or to someone else's, or being something like a father—an uncle, a mentor, a coach, a teacher, a therapist—is the real way to become a man. We gain our masculinity not by waving it from flagpoles or measuring and testing it before cheering crowds but by teaching it to boys and girls, and to men and women who haven't known a man up close and don't know what men and masculinity are all about. If men would raise children, it would not only save the world in a generation or two, it would save their lives."

- Frank Pittman, *Man Enough*

The plan worked in part but failed in the more important parts. While I was able to attract clients and work their legal cases to pay the bills, the school for the children fell through at the last moment, and I could see they felt stranded, so far from our family in the south of the state.

I always kept the door to my bedroom open, and I became a grief counselor and trauma therapist to my older children (as I had learned to do from my own counselors). I tried to date, but that was a disaster each time. Some of my older kids came up with what was for them a very funny game of finding *much* older women on internet dating sites, calling me over to check out these potential matches and breaking into sidesplitting laughter as they watched my reactions.

After I informed them I would no longer play this game, they begged me to give them one more chance, asking me to start by telling them what she "needed to look like." I sarcastically responded: "Okay, I want her to look like Reese Witherspoon—including her dimples."

We had relative peace in the house for a couple of weeks until one night, my kids invited me to come out of my room and see whom they had found. I reluctantly came out, fully expecting another joke, especially since they announced they had found Reese Witherspoon's lookalike. As I approached the computer screen, I was shocked to see they were not playing games: the woman staring back at me from the screen was beautiful, blonde, and had dimples like Reese Witherspoon!

So, I sat down and read the profile of a 35-year-old single woman, Kari Tank, who had never been married and had no children. I immediately thought, *She will certainly not be willing to date a man with nine children!* I also thought that, at 35 years old, this younger woman might be able to have children. The thought of adding to my nine kids exhilarated and scared me at the same time!

I reached out and, in a story that is too long for telling here, we connected. Eventually, Kari came to help me school the children, since their original school plans had failed, and after a year of dating, we were married on Christmas Day 2009, much to the chagrin, at the time, of the older children.

I have to say that, during this time, I felt like a failure as a father, and kept looking for ways to decrease the burden on my children. I learned so much about children during this period: not only how resilient they are, but also how loving and forgiving they are. They probably comforted me more than I comforted them!

To our great surprise and delight, Kari and I conceived a honeymoon baby, our little Cajetan. Four more followed, as well as two miscarriages, whom we named and claimed. Including Jackie's one miscarriage, this brought the number of children God entrusted us to 17. As I write this, the first seven have left the nest. And, while the pang of missing them continues to touch me, I know our children must grow up and fly. I simply invite Jesus into these feelings of loss, and He transforms them into love.

As of this writing, we are about to welcome our eleventh and twelfth grandchildren into the world. As I look back over my life, its ups and downs, twists and turns, I am constantly reminded that we were not put on this earth for ourselves, but for others. If we have spouses, it is our duty to help them along the road to Heaven and to mold and raise our children in the ways of the faith so they too might enjoy eternal life with Christ for eternity!

DAVID HAEFS

David Haefs is an Army veteran currently employed at Lockheed Martin in Texas, where he grew up and now resides with his family. He and his wife Ali have been married for 20 years and have three daughters and two sons. David enjoys anything outdoors, campfires, swimming, playing board games and Lego building with his kids. The family has 25 animals, homeschools, and is very thankful for all the extra time they can spend together as a family.

A Father's Hands

On October 9, 2020, my 15-year-old daughter, Kayla, was diagnosed with Stage 4 Hodgkin's lymphoma. Eight days after beginning chemotherapy, Kayla collapsed outside of our home. She was rushed to the hospital by ambulance with severe abdominal pain and a white blood cell count of nearly zero. After a couple of hours, we learned her body had gone into sepsis. She was intubated, given plasma and platelets, and within 24 hours, had to undergo emergency surgery to remove part of her colon. Within another 24 hours, Kayla's heart was weakened to the point of requiring life support on an ECMO machine. At that time, we were told she had a 30 percent chance of living.

My wife, Ali, and I stood reeling from all that was taking place completely beyond our control. Why was this happening? What did God want? Did He *actually* want to take our little girl? We had no say about the cancer that had invaded Kayla's

just want her healed so I can take her home … I'm struggling with trusting the doctors… Help me until morning."

During this time, I (and many others) cried a lot of tears and desperate prayers. All I could really do was hold my baby's hand. As a man, I take comfort in being a protector and provider. I hate feeling out of control, especially when it comes to the health and safety of my family. And during this time, that power was stripped from me.

Finally, one night in the hospital chapel, I came to a breaking point. I cried out to the Lord, "Whatever the outcome, I trust in You!"

This was a terrifying, gut-wrenching prayer to pray, but I meant it! And afterwards, I had a sweet peace and comforting spirit come over me.

I reflected in my journal: "Man is not the answer. The beeps on the machines are not a worry. The numbers are not a stress. You are in control. I will trust in You."

It took what felt like an eternity for Kayla to show signs of improvement. She was on life support for 10 days. During the process, she also had a seizure and suffered a stroke.

body. We had no power to determine how her system was responding to chemo treatments. We had no professional knowledge of medical machines or emergency procedures. We felt helpless: our daughter's life was in the hands of others.

One of my journal entries from this time captures some of my emotions: "God, it is heartbreaking and numbing to see Kayla in the condition she is in. I

But through surgeries, tubes, treatments, and a ton of prayer, the life-and-death crisis was averted!

Kayla still had many rounds of chemo to complete. She spent a month on the physical therapy floor, relearning almost everything: standing, walking, feeding herself. But on December 23, after nearly two months in the hospital, we were finally and miraculously able to bring Kayla home. By the end of March, she had completed her treatment and was officially *cancer free*!

It has been over two years since the diagnosis and the terrible events that followed. We praise God for the healing and salvation He showed us. We also remind ourselves to walk the road of trust and dependence every day. Kayla still has braces on her legs. The full repair of her nerves is uncertain, and we often wish we could control the pace of her recovery.

But God reminds me He can be trusted. I'm not helpless; I'm helped. And my family is most secure in our Father's hands.

"Do not be anxious about anything, but in every situation, by prayer and petition, with thanksgiving, present your requests to God. And the peace of God, which transcends all understanding, will guard your hearts and your minds in Christ Jesus""

– Philippians 4:6-7

23

JOSHUA SHASSERRE

Joshua Shasserre and his wife, Nikki, have been married for 19 years and have six children, relying on the intercession of their seventh already in Heaven. Josh is currently an attorney in the Nebraska Attorney General's office and teaches undergraduate business law at the University of Nebraska.

Answering the Call

"We have a little girl who needs to be placed in emergency foster care," began the phone call I received a dozen years ago.

The little girl, Cathy, was in the second-grade class taught by my sister-in-law. Six years into our marriage, we had not yet been blessed with children. Could we truly care for a seven-year-old child? Could we bear to give her back? We embraced the risk and responded to the call to love.

The next eight months challenged our answers to both questions until another call came from our caseworker, who said

Cathy's biological father was relinquishing his parental rights. I wept tears of joy when I called my wife on her birthday to tell her we would soon be able to adopt Cathy.

A few months after deciding to become foster parents, we were approached by a friend who assisted women in crisis pregnancies about our willingness to adopt an infant. As we celebrated our first Christmas with Cathy, we all awaited the birth of her little sister. On New Year's Eve, we received word that the baby girl we planned to adopt was born, but we would not be her parents.

In February, my wife was contacted by a former colleague asking for prayers for a family with a teenage daughter considering adoption. After one failed adoption, I was not willing to embrace the risk, but my wife instinctively reached out to respond with a call of love. The colleague asked us to be adoptive parents again, and two weeks later, we received the call that Aidan was soon to be born. Aidan's open adoption has given us an additional family that has enriched our lives immeasurably.

Two years later, we were blessed by our first pregnancy. Our Elizabeth was miraculously born despite my wife suffering with 13 fibroids. Next came Samuel, our fourth child, making us a "big family." Then came the most excruciating call to trust in God's love: the ultrasound technician told us our son Simon's heartbeat could not be found. He now intercedes for us from Heaven, giving us even more motivation to be fully with him again. God later blessed us with twins, Corbella and Luke.

The world tempts men to ignore the call to care for others, to take risks to further their career but avoid the risk to grow in sacrificial love. Today, I respond to the call of "Dad" in myriad ways, some of which I am still not great at responding to.

"Dad, will you please share my hot dog pizza?"

"Dad, will you help me with my algebra homework?"

"Dad, I'm pregnant."

Admittedly, this last statement was one I was least prepared for, thinking Cathy was sure to complete college. But as new grandparents, we now happily respond to calls like, "Mom and Dad, the baby is fussy. What do I do?"

Experiencing the daily reward of a messy, exuberant, challenging, joyful, and abundant family, I am grateful to have been granted the grace to respond to the call.

24

CARLOS CORDON

Carlos Cordon is a happy husband and endocrine surgeon with a master's degree in Public Health. He lives in Guatemala with his wife and five children, which "pairs well" with his passion for wine as a sommelier.

I married young. At age 24. When I still was a medical student.

And so began our adventure. Like everyone else, we have had ups and downs, joys and sorrows. Life has dealt hard blows, but they have united my wife and me and forged us as a couple.

My first child was born almost halfway through my internship—madness, some will think. But spontaneity and surprises spice up life! It was hard, of course, but the happiness and excitement of having my first child outweighed the difficulties. During my long hours working in the hospital, I missed my son, but the simple fact of remembering I had a baby, my son,

at home, filled me with joy and made it easier for me.

I had no idea that by the time I finished my studies to be a surgeon, I would have five children.

I never considered or planned how many I would have, so each child was a surprise, a pleasant surprise. It is the most wonderful experience there is. There is no manual on how to educate children, especially when we see how even in the same house, the same habits and traditions form such different children.

It is impossible to talk about my experience as a father without including my wife, Mercy, especially when in multiple crises, I was on call or in the hospital and she had to figure things out on her own.

While we had no manual, Mercy and I did not make decisions thoughtlessly. We agreed on how to raise the children and also had immense help from our church, which guided us with courses and talks that helped us make the best decisions. And when things were particularly difficult, we always had the unconditional support of the priests, who were at our disposal 24/7.

Now the children are adults, and I have a different relationship with them. I am proud to see, despite my 54 years, that I have much to learn from each of them. One child is methodical, disciplined, meticulous. Another is stoic and resilient in difficult situations. I have one who is persistent and constant, yet wildly spontaneous. The son who grew up to be an architect looks at life very differently, and it is practically impossible to see him angry; there is no rancor in his life. He always sees the funny side of things, even in complicated situations.

My daughter, the only one among four men, is the darling of the family. We wondered how this might affect her—being everyone's "princess"—but it obviously served her well as she turned out to be no-nonsense, practical, and efficient.

Would I repeat this same story if I had the chance? Of course. I wouldn't trade it for any other story in the world.

25

JIM HINES

Jim Hines is a dad to two special sons, Brendan (30) and Brian (28). Although no longer married, he readily shares, "I am very close to my former spouse, who is an incredible mom to our sons." He was "the candy man" for 31 years in sales for Mars, Inc., selling M&M's, Snickers, 3 Musketeers, Starburst, Skittles, Milky Way, and many others. In retirement, he enjoys the extra time he can spend with his sons while remaining active in local community events and advocacy for people with disabilities.

Like most first-time fathers, I thought I had an idea of what was in front of me. Little did I know how completely ill-equipped and unprepared I was for the job of raising Brendan and Brian. After coming home from the hospital after our first son's birth, I was busy calling friends sharing the great news!

Then the phone rang: Brendan's mother was in tears, informing me he was suffering seizures. I went from the euphoric feeling of fatherhood to the sheer terror of wondering what the future held for Brendan. Within hours, doctors informed us Brendan's life would be very difficult.

We soon became too familiar with the neonatal intensive care unit at Mary Bridge Children's Hospital. Subsequently, ambulance rides, therapy, diagnostic procedures, and hospitalizations became the norm.

Genetic testing provided us with confidence about expanding our young family. God had other plans. Brian was born two years later and began seizing six hours after birth. When it began, I crumpled into a corner with a towel and began to cry. I couldn't imagine what this meant for our future. We were yet again thrust into a world of biopsies, neurology, and the great unknown.

However, this bumpy and beautiful journey has allowed me to become something bigger and better. While my boys cannot speak like you and me, their smiles and happy noises are the light of my life. Because of Brendan and Brian's unique characteristics, I have become more compassionate, empathetic, and generous.

I've been blessed to serve on multiple boards of directors, including Mary Bridge Children's Foundation, Special Olympics, and National Organization Caring for Kids. Further, I have found myself onstage emceeing multiple charity events. None of these opportunities to serve would be possible without God's gifts, Brendan and Brian.

Our family life has never been easy, but I wouldn't trade my boys for anything or anyone. God has graced us with two perfect souls. Also benefiting from Brendan and Brian's pure innocence are our nine unbelievable caregivers, who serve God by coming into our homes and lives. I'm not sure what I did to deserve this, but my gratitude knows no bounds.

Thank you, Brendan and Brian. Thank you too, Lord Jesus.

"The rain came down,
the streams rose,
and the winds blew
and beat against that house;
yet it did not fall,
because it had its foundation
on the rock."

– Matthew 7:25

26

TOM CARMODY

Tom Carmody is a retired small business owner in the Seattle area. He and his wife, Lori, combine his business talents with her spiritual direction gifts to grow the faith of young adults by helping to form a Young Catholic Professionals chapter in the Archdiocese of Seattle.
www.youngcatholicprofessionals.org

After six years of dating and five years of marriage, my wife Lori and I decided we were ready to have children. We wanted three or four kids. God had other plans.

We spent the next four years trying to conceive. Our doctor warned us our chances for a baby were slim to none, but we kept the faith and were finally blessed with a beautiful baby boy. We named him Matthew ("gift from God"). I couldn't have been happier.

Fatherhood was everything I dreamed of and more. It wasn't long after Matthew started drinking out of a sippy cup that we decided to try for another. One month led to another. One year led to another.

Again, our plans were not God's.

We had considered adoption before Lori had conceived, and she was open to it again. I was open to it before Matthew but was no longer interested due to concerns of being able to love my adopted child as much as my biological child. Lori never pressured me. We both prayed, trusting we would come to consensus one way or the other.

While shopping for Lori's birthday, I was in a Christian bookstore and could not find a gift. But there was a plaque on the shelf I kept coming back to. I saw no particular significance to it beyond it being a hopeful message. It was a verse from Jeremiah: "For I know the plans I have for you … plans to give you hope and a future" (Jeremiah 29:11). I bought it.

After a few other gifts, Lori unwrapped the plaque. When she saw it, she started to cry. I was confused. Imagine my surprise when I learned that Jeremiah 29:11 was the verse that consoled her in prayer whenever she was feeling sad about our conception-versus-adoption dilemma.

It wasn't long before my heart shifted about adoption. We were in our late thirties, and entered what felt like a lottery. The chances we would be picked by a pregnant woman with an average age of 20 was quite low. After all, we weren't much younger than the expectant mother's parents. We made the odds even worse by requesting a newborn girl. We learned most of the young women our agency worked with were low income, and prenatal care was limited. Most did not know the sex of their child until birth, and the agency wanted them to choose the adoptive parents weeks before birth. Plus, we already had a biological son. We were told biological moms

tended to want to place their child with an infertile couple. It was a long shot, but we kept the faith.

A year later, we received the phone call. A baby girl was born to a mother our age. The birth mother had an eight-year-old son (about the age of our son) whom she had previously placed up for adoption. Because the baby was born premature, the birth mother hadn't received the profiles of adoptive parents from which to choose. Realizing it was a girl, and knowing a decision hadn't been made, the agency sent her one more profile, ours, and we were chosen!

We drove five hours to the hospital and met our newborn little girl in the NICU. We named her Kaitie Ann ("pure grace").

I could not have been happier. We were able to feed her, and then back into the incubator she went.

We were thrilled. We found some dinner and were heading back to the hotel when we had the urge to go to church to give thanks. This was in the days before GPS. Not being familiar with the town, I took a few lefts and a right, and there was a church with an empty parking lot. We hopped out of the car to check if the door was unlocked, and saw that not only was the building open, but it was a Catholic church! We proceeded inside toward the altar, knelt, and prayed. We were so happy, so grateful.

It wasn't a long visit. On the way out, on the back wall near the exit, we noticed a beautifully framed sculpture of Jesus holding his cupped hands out toward us. Next to it was a plaque with a Scripture verse on it: "For I know the plans I have for you… plans to give you hope and a future."

Our little girl is now 27 years old and a fifth-grade schoolteacher at a Catholic grade school, the very one she attended. I am grateful for my wife, who showed me patience. She has made me a better dad. As for my old fear, I assure everyone who asks that I cannot tell the difference between the deep fatherly love I have for my biological son, Matthew, and the deep fatherly love I have for my adopted daughter, Kaitie Ann.

Our plans were good. His plans were better.

27

LUIS PEDRO PEREZ

Luis, a father of four, is a periodontist who was born and raised in Guatemala, and enjoys, in his spare time, being a dragon fruit hobby farmer.

Being a father is one of the most extraordinary experiences in life. You become a father with the experiences you have loved from your own childhood. I had an amazing example with my dad, who, while not a perfect man, was the perfect father to me. He taught me numerous things that made me who I am today.

So then, you apply what you learned as a child, and you try to do it even better, if possible.

Something key for me was to find the right woman, and I found the best person for this project of life was Luisa, my wife. She polished and improved what I brought with me, and together we have four kids (one already in Heaven), who, with their qualities and challenges, make us an extraordinary family.

When a baby arrives, it's always an immense and indescribable joy. With Santiago, our first, like most first-time parents, Luisa and I tended to overprotect and worried for every little thing. I remember Luisa would put a mirror close to his mouth when he was sleeping to check that he was breathing. Today, Santiago has an immense heart, and sometimes he doesn't even know it.

The second one was supposed to be easier, but God took her to His side early. With great sadness we delivered our stillborn daughter, Natalia. I'm sure she is taking care of us from Heaven.

Our third, a precious girl, Cristy, was born with special needs, and developed Multiple Sclerosis in her teen years. This brought us to sleepless nights and endless tears, thinking that our world was over. But thanks be to God, Cristy is a fighter and continues to strive, and enriches our lives with the joy she carries.

With Martin, our fourth, we are way more relaxed, as one is with the last ones. He amuses us with his sense of humor and spirited character.

As time goes by, as a dad, I've lived the joys and sorrows that any family experiences. It is important to not get too focused on the problems. After all, that could distract our view of the wonderful life God gave us when He made us parents!

God doesn't stop the bad things from happening;
that's never been part of the promise. The promise is:
'I am with you. I am with you now until the end of time.'

– Madeleine L'Engle

PART 4

Grit and Glory

Love what you do, and you'll never work a day in your life. I've heard this mantra for a long time. Tricky phrase.

You might interpret it like, *Find your passion—find a job that is your passion—and you'll never work a day, because you'll love what you do so much, you won't think it's work.*

Hmmm…

For some, yes, that could be true.

For most, no. That's an illusion.

My dad loves what he does.

My husband loves his work.

Was it their passion from the beginning, or did they fall in love passionately with their jobs while working?

My dad applied to Pedodontics (Children's Dentistry) in Oregon while studying in New York. Doing an interview over the phone, his accent was so strong they thought he was saying Periodontics (Gums). When he got to Oregon, he was received with open arms to the "Department of Periodontics." After he recovered from his surprise, he shrugged his shoulders, and thought, *Perio it is!* And he absolutely and completely loved

his profession. He went to work until he was 93 with a smile on his face.

I think happiness is finding joy wherever you are, whatever you're doing—doing your best and giving it all for the love of others.

This sounds to me like what a father does.

I don't think anyone is born with a passion to change diapers, for endless nights trying to get a baby to sleep, or talking to a teenager who needs that time, a passion to see your child struggle, a passion to correct, without any success a lot of the time, with a passion to work all day and come home, breathe in, breath out, and cross that door where chaos awaits. I think you find yourself with all these on your lap, and you *make* it your passion. And then, you love it. And then, you invite God into your plans, and you let Him change them, anyway He pleases.

That's living. Living passionately, loving the world.

And that's a dad.

~Manola Secaira

95

28

JONATHAN CONRAD

Jonathan Conrad, "the Catholic Woodworker," grew up building things with his dad and grandfather. He is married to his high-school sweetheart, Carey, and they are blessed with three boys. Jonathan says his zeal for daily prayer, the rosary, and the sacraments fuels everything he does as a husband, father, and son of God.

On Control, Fatherhood, and the Lies

If I could use my skill as a woodworker to be a better father, it would look like this: Plan the size and shape of fortitude, faith, love, leadership, and patience. Cut them out. Strengthen and repair the flaws in the material with the Sacraments. Sand them down to reveal the real manhood. Chisel out the childhood wounds, bad choices, and crippling fears. Join all the pieces together using God's grace. Engrave God's commandments on his heart. And finish with a coat of holiness.

And *voilà*! A perfect Catholic father!

I wish it were that simple.

You see, I have all these ideas and inspirations about how to bring the faith into my relationship with my children, how to teach them about the faith, and how to walk with them in their faith journeys. I have this ardent desire for them to know God and serve Him when they're adults.

But I find myself making all these excuses: *I don't know how to teach people. I don't know how to be a mentor. I don't know how to control the outcome.*

Then doubts creep in: *What if I'm not good enough? What if I'm not leading them in the faith? What if they choose to leave the faith?*

Before I've even started, I've already failed.

So, I unpacked all these doubts—and here's what I found …

Firstly, it's a lie that I don't know how to teach. When I say it out loud, it even *sounds* ridiculous. I'm a dad. I have some experience being a mentor. I've been a mentor to my eldest son for 12 years. I mentor people at work.

The thing is, I can control work, or at least I feel like I can control work. So going after something at work doesn't scare me because I'm confident I can be successful. But I hesitate sometimes when it comes to bringing the faith into my relationship with my children. I realize that despite my best efforts, the future is not up to me. Discouragement can defeat me before I set foot on the battlefield.

I look at all these "great Catholics" who have a public life that's shared on the internet, and I compare myself to them. I look at all the things they *do* as Catholic fathers, and judge myself inadequate and my efforts, insufficient. And because I don't do *those* same fatherly things, I've already disqualified myself. So the things I feel inspired to do are counteracted by this lie that I've already failed.

At the same time, I'm aware that if I give in to the discouragement, or believe this lie, then my kids won't have a relationship with God. And if they don't, what's *that* going to mean about my identity?

But praise God for these truths!

God is not asking me to be this *other* person on the internet. He's asking me to be me—uniquely called and capable—a father and steward of these children, my children. My calling is not about anyone else's kids in any other home, parish, community, or in any other country for that matter. I'm called to be Jonathan Conrad, husband to my wife and father to our three boys.

God gave my children the freedom to choose. They get to choose how to love God. Isn't that a beautiful part of who they are, that they get to make that choice? They're going to relate to God however they choose to. And get this: He will still love them no matter what they choose. That means I am free to do the same.

My sons will not have the same faith I have, thanks be to God. I can't expect my three boys to have the same relationship with God, any more than two saints are similar; God made each one of us unique.

God's love and mercy bring me back in spite of everything I fail to do, in spite of the lies and temptation to self-reliance and in spite of the things my own parents did or failed to do.

I'm not perfect, and it's okay.

I announce the truth that while I am finite, God is infinite. My patience and wisdom are limited, but God's love is limitless and His mercies are tender and new every morning.

I can focus on the things that I can control: how I show up for my children, how I love them, and how I share my personal relationship with God to my boys.

It's never too late to hear God's truths, and I can always start again.

29

BRET FRANCESCONI

Bret Francesconi has been married to his wife for 17 years is the father of two boys. He is a school counselor, incredible chef, and innovative home bartender.

Being a parent is hard work. Nobody is ever fully prepared for the opportunity, but it is a blessing. To parent a child is to be given the gift to mold clay like God did when He created us. The things you invest in, say, and do are mimicked and eventually become the foundation on which children live their lives.

Sometimes we see the things we love about ourselves in our children, and sometimes not. I often think about these things, even the silly ones. For example, when I stub my toe on something and get that excruciating "I want to scream but I won't" feeling. I hop around the house and tell everyone to not talk to me. Then one day, my son did the exact same routine, and I thought, *Uh oh, is that what I look like?* I laughed, but I also felt embarrassed at what I created. But I adjusted my behavior the next time. Lesson learned. Move forward.

Being a stubborn father can often backfire as well. I probably have a single-spaced, hundred-page list of examples of this. One time, when my youngest was around age four (he is more stubborn than I am), I had a stare-down moment with him on whether or not he was going to eat his dinner: a plain cheese quesadilla. He said "No," and I said, "Eat it or else."

At this juncture, you can imagine what I might have said, but I was beyond convincing him how important the food was for him, so I said something like, "Eat it or I'll have the doctor explain to you why you need to eat your dinner." At this point, I recalled some wisdom that stated, "You have to stand by your word, or your kids won't respect you for it." Well—*gulp*—the words were out. After several more exchanges between the two of us, I threw him over my shoulder, grabbed the quesadilla and my car keys, marched down the stairs, and hopped in the car. Once buckled, I turned the engine on in hopes that he would eat it, but he didn't.

Well, shoot, I thought. *I'm going to have to go through with this.*

Putting the car in reverse, I looked over my shoulder, released the brake pedal … and found myself looking back at a child shoving a quesadilla in his mouth so fast, I wondered

if he even breathed. Did I win? Yes. I won the Most Stubborn Award… that is, until I realized what I gained from this.

A lesson learned is a wisdom gained. To be stubborn is to make a choice without wisdom, and God wants us to lead by healthy examples so we can have our children's trust in those moments they really need us.

Fast forward a few years, and this same child, after bedtime prayer, asked me why he didn't hear from God. Talk about catching you when you least expect it! I explained how I had moments when I felt close to God and moments I felt I couldn't hear Him. This seemed to settle him for that time, but after thinking it out more and talking with my wife (there is always wisdom in talking to your spouse), we thought we would present it to one of the pastors of our church. We let our son choose who he thought would be best, and then he and I went to meet with that pastor separately. The pastor was delighted to be presented with this question and gave my son a task: to read the Bible on his own. He was to start with the four Gospels, getting my support along the way. The pastor said that often, when he wanted to hear from God, he turned to the Bible. I'll tell you, that kid took that advice and ran with it! He read those four Gospels and kept going. I was delighted when I watched him take to this.

Fatherhood is a journey, but one you do together with your spouse, your kids, and most importantly, with God. He is the ultimate and best example of fatherhood. When Christ was ready to begin His mission, God called down from on high and told everyone, "This is my son, whom I love; with him I am well pleased" (Matthew 3:17). Remind your kids daily of this message. I try day and night to remind my own kids they are loved and important. At the end of the day, they are not ours. They are His.

"No man stands taller than when he stoops to help a child."

– Abraham Lincoln

30

THOMAS JONSSON

Thomas Jonsson was born in Sundsvall, Sweden and grew up in Sweden, Spain, and France. He earned a master's degree in Industrial Engineering and Economics from the University of Linköping. He met his wife in Spain and they have been married 38 years. Their first five children were born abroad in Madrid, Spain, and the last two in Portland, Oregon. Currently, Thomas and his wife live and work out of the island of Puerto Rico.

I didn't plan fatherhood: it planned *me*. I am now a father to seven incredible human beings and grandfather to one—at least for the time being. The ages of our two daughters and five sons range between 18 and 36 years old. I can honestly say this is something I never imagined, let alone planned, when my wife and I were married nearly 38 years ago. And today I look back and realize fatherhood planned me because I am not who I thought I would be when we embarked on the journey of building a family.

Time is relentless, but it is kind. Kids come one by one—or sometimes as twins or triplets, of course—and God does not give us the grace for what we will be going through in five, 10, 15, or 20 years: He gives us grace for the moment. If you don't take the chance, you miss the adventure. So when people look at me aghast and ask how I managed seven kids, I laugh it off and say, "After four, my wife and I lost control, because we only had four hands between the two of us!"

Sometimes, I will tell them that the funny thing is, after four kids, things changed for the better. And that I don't regret a single thing. It changed me as a person: "I" took a back seat. I began to trust that my wife and I were in this together and that we would be successful if we also learned to be better along the way.

Without a doubt, family and close friends contribute extra help and limbs when needed. Looking back now, I can say with certainty it takes a big village to raise a child. And that while plans will often work out, we are never in *complete* control.

All through the years, we've found humor and moral support in what is written on two magnets on our fridge door. They both were slogans that helped us survive and thrive in a home with kids, family, friends that became like our kids, continuously moving schedules, and a bit of organized chaos wherever you looked. The first one reads: "We plan and God laughs," and the second one goes: "You cannot scare us. We have teenagers."

Hey, I can safely say that today I am a far braver and somewhat wiser man than I was 36 years ago. And that is because, as I said, fatherhood gave me far more than I put into it. Fatherhood planned me.

ANTONIO SECAIRA

Antonio Secaira is an interventional cardiologist, creative mixologist, and avid outdoorsman who is passionate about adventures, whether in the water or the mountains. He was born and raised in Guatemala and now lives in Tacoma, Washington, where he and his wife Manola have raised their eight children.

I stepped into fatherhood without fully understanding it—I think most of us do. As a young man, I do not think I fully grasped the responsibilities involved with this task, and it took me well into my years as a father to start understanding the idea.

As the author John Green said, "The nature of impending fatherhood is that you are doing something that you're unqualified to do, and then you become qualified while doing it."

Fatherhood has been a great adventure. As father of three young women and five young men, I can say that it has been a journey.

With no instruction manual and just some basic principles to go by, fatherhood is a "train-on-the-job" experience, and maybe that is why each kid turns out so differently.

There is no one way to do it right, but there certainly are ways to do it wrong. This idea sometimes keeps me up at night. I am not talking about the little problems, like losing my temper or missing a game or a school play. I mean the important stuff, the stuff that builds character and forms a person. Often, we teach children the important stuff by what we do rather than what we say to them.

Early on, I realized that little children, even before a year of age, are like sponges that absorb anything and everything in their environment.

As a dad, I know I am flawed. For many years, I tried to be the strong person, the wise person I thought my children needed. I tried to hide my own shortcomings, simultaneously demanding more of them than what I was able to give at their age.

One of my goals was to take responsibility for these little ones and make them far better beings than I am.

There is a certain age when the father is no longer the strong person who has a solution for everything in the eyes of his children. This may be difficult for some to accept, but nevertheless, it is the natural order of things. At that time, there may be more conflicts and clashes with our children: they want (and have) to make their own decisions and mistakes—and youth dictates they do it with bravado.

Here is perhaps when we can make a bigger difference. Instead of trying to be strong and knowledgeable, our kids need to see both our vulnerable side *and* our

resolve to overcome. They need to see our resilience during adversity and our humility to accept what is not under our control with the attitude that allows us to play the "long game." We should instill the attitude to work toward a better future and the reassuring truth that as long as we are together and the family is strong, we will endure whatever storms come our way.

To young fathers, I would advise this: Don't sweat the little things. Be the man your family needs: that alone is a full-time job and a journey. Be humble, be loving, and be forgiving. Be as forgiving with yourself as you are with others. *Especially* with yourself, because mistakes will happen; things can be done better, and what was good today may not be advisable tomorrow.

I am still learning from my children; the younger ones are not any easier and come with new challenges I am still trying to work out.

As I move toward grandfatherhood, I think things will be easier...but then again, this seems to be yet another job I'll learn on the go. I guess I will figure it out when I get there. Wish me luck.

KEN MAUERMANN

Ken Mauermann has had a lifelong passion for trains! From train hopping as a teen, guiding tours, and even leading the development for a new community train station, his enchantment with trains that first stirred in his heart as a boy has never diminished. Ken worked for the Washington State Department of Ecology  and for Tacoma Electric. Ken has thoroughly enjoyed the ride of raising his two sons with his wife, Sue, and teaching their grandchildren how to train hop—amongst other adventures!

Fatherhood. When I stop to think about it and really delve into the last 40 years, it almost seems unreal. It has been a remarkable experience, filled with its share of triumphs and challenges.

I remember the day we brought our firstborn home from the hospital. It wasn't until that short drive home that the reality of being responsible for another human being hit me. Up until that time, I knew our pregnancy would result in a life-changing experience, but it still felt distant, out there in the future somewhere. Suddenly, the future was here, and there now was somebody in that new car seat that had until now ridden unoccupied and relatively unnoticed in the back seat of the car. I remember feeling somewhat helpless, trying to share the new responsibilities with my wife to lessen her burden. Cooking and cleaning weren't anything new. Tending to the baby's myriad needs was obviously uncharted territory, but I was determined to do my part in any way I could. Regardless, the bulk of the work fell unfairly on Mom. (I was secretly thankful I was unable to breastfeed.)

The arrival of our second son was *so* much easier. The learning curve in caring for a newborn had been considerably shortened. My duties largely entailed keeping tabs on our two-year-old while Mom tended to the new arrival. By then, I was stroller trained and feeling a whole lot more comfortable with having another brand-new baby in our lives. I wasn't up and down all night just to make sure the little guy was still breathing. Mom had most of that all-night shift as, once again, I fell short when it came to breastfeeding.

Flash forward. Suddenly, there was baseball, soccer, cross-country, school functions, and parent conferences. There were scheduling difficulties, but we were determined parents and those things were priorities. I remember that whenever social functions arose, we navigated our way to those that included the kids. My own dad had included me in most facets of daily life, so I did the same. When I was working around the house or out in the garage, I took the time to show the boys what I was doing and let them "help" when possible to teach self-sufficiency. That was more important than it seemed at the time, as both boys are now capable do-it-yourself-ers.

As I look back, I am proud of how my guys turned out despite some rough terrain along the way. No question, it was not all roses and sunshine. I'm not sure how, but both kids display more common sense than I ever had and an amazing work ethic. Both have successful careers, and most importantly, both are fathers deeply involved with their own children. Like we did, they are bent on instilling in their kids a sense of right and wrong, integrity, and an awareness of the sensitivities of others. As their father, watching them emphasize these things to their kids makes me incredibly proud of what personal attributes we were able to give our boys. It makes me realize the value of what my father gave to me.

Prayer of Saint Francis

Lord, make me an instrument of your peace.
Where there is hatred, let me bring love.
Where there is offense, let me bring pardon.
Where there is discord, let me bring union.
Where there is error, let me bring truth.
Where there is doubt, let me bring faith.
Where there is despair, let me bring hope.
Where there is darkness, let me bring your light.
Where there is sadness, let me bring joy.
O Master, let me not seek as much to be consoled as to console,
to be understood as to understand, to be loved as to love, for it
is in giving that one receives, it is in self forgetting that one finds,
it is in pardoning that one is pardoned,
it is in dying that one is raised to eternal life.

DAVE WHITESELL

Dave Whitesell celebrates 25 years of marriage this year to his wife, Shelly. They have seven children here on Earth and three waiting for them up in Heaven. Dave graduated with his bachelor's degree in business from Northwest University, and a master's level certification in church management. Dave has worked for the archdiocese of Seattle in a variety of positions since becoming Catholic in 2003. Starting out in youth ministry, he currently serves as the parish administrator at St. Frances Cabrini Parish in Lakewood, Washington. Dave has a passion for soccer and coaches a local boys' premiere soccer team. If he isn't busy with "dad duties," running crazy at the parish, or out on the soccer pitch coaching, you will occasionally find him fishing.

Most people have regrets. Regrets are good. They show a person has learned, that we are aware our mistakes have consequences. Sometimes, those consequences last a lifetime. Many of us are blessed to embrace those regrets. I strive to every day. They help me become a better person.

My regrets may sound a tad crazy. Two of my biggest regrets are over things that were out of my control. First, I so wish my wife and I were blessed with more children. Second, I wish I had learned to have more patience a lot sooner. To understand the irony of these regrets, you need a little background.

We were blessed with 10 children. The good Lord gave us seven children here on Earth. Three of our children are waiting for us up in Heaven. I can't wait to see them, give them big hugs, and get to know them. The irony is that when my wife and I were courting and even after our wedding, I didn't want *any* children. God forbid I had more than one child, Lord have mercy if I had two or more! I had plans of my own—big plans. Children weren't in my plans. This now makes me laugh hysterically—well, and cry. The level of hubris and selfishness I possessed as a young man was pathetic. I laugh at my youthful years. I've heard it said, "If you want to make God laugh, tell Him your plans."

The moment I held my first child, looked into her precious face, cut her umbilical cord, and gently washed the vernix coating from her skin, I was hooked. Her crying sounded like angelic singing. Her need for food and incessant pooping filled my days with greater understanding and purpose. Isn't that hilarious? Crying, feeding, and pooping brought a strapping, athletic, cocky young man to deeper understanding and purpose. Seven children later—three college graduates, one high schooler going off to play college soccer on

scholarship, and three left in the house—and all I can usually think about is how deeply I wish we could have raised the three I never met, and many more. Call me selfish, crazy, or both.

I was and am a strict disciplinarian. I don't regret that. Children need discipline. In fact, they yearn for it. That said, discipline must be practiced alongside love and patience. They must be values you cling to as a father. I am a man who loves very deeply but being patient is something I struggle with to this day.

At a certain point in my life, I had a four-year-old, a three-year-old, and a two-year-old. One morning, I awoke to quite the surprise. I came walking down the stairs to two of them doing the dishes. Cute, right? *No!* This wasn't cute at all. They were doing the dishes with sugar and flour … all over our kitchen floor. They thought the sugar and flour were dish soap. I wish I could tell you that I was a cool dad. That I sat down with them, right in the middle of that mess, finished up "washing the dishes," and then cleaned up. No, I did not. I lost it. I yelled, "What are you doing?! No!"

I so wish I could have that moment and many more back. I regret snapping at my children, and that regret will stay with me a lifetime. However, I also see how that regret has shaped my character and made me a better man, husband, father, and grandfather. I can't go back and have more children. And I can't take a time machine back to that crisp fall morning two of my little ones decided to help me with the dishes. But I can embrace every day and thank God for making me a father. It is the second-greatest blessing in my life.

What's the first, you may wonder? Well, the Lord blessed me with my wife as well!

PART 5

Love without End

My dad would whistle a tune every time he came in through the door after work, and set himself in a steady position to grab running kids that would leap to his arms (that is, until we were too big to continue the leap without injuring him!).

My husband would carry four kids up the stairs to bed: two on his back, and two on his arms, while I would watch the sweet sight while feeding our newborn fifth child.

Watching a dad be a horse with kids on his back, a monster chasing them around the house, or a bear, crawling to find kids hiding, can be a beautiful insight into the world of fatherhood. It is in this play—after work, tired, worried at times, when everything else disappears except for the needs of the family—that we can see a spark of the generosity of a dad. It is there, where they are laying "cruciform" on the floor, that they are giving everything they have, and, even when there is nothing left, still giving more.

My dad would wake up before anyone to study his periodontics journal; I never knew why so early. My husband gets up before anyone, to work out. That way he doesn't "steal" family time. Now I understand why my dad was such an early riser. When we would all wake up, he was ready for the day, like nothing had transpired before that moment. Without saying anything to anyone.

The father, the protector. I love this adjective for a man. There are so many other ones that can describe a dad. Yet, "the protector" covers so much more than what that word means at first glance. "Protector" doesn't mean "savior." It doesn't mean perfect either. It means *present*.

It means not knowing what to do when the load gets very heavy, when the problems grow bigger than humanly possible to bear. It means not knowing what to do, what to say, or where to begin, but being willing to simply be. To stand there next to the son/daughter and love them. This is a dad. Rolling up his sleeves, and getting "muddy," sometimes without any strength, sometimes with all the wisdom and fortitude possible. Sometimes looking at his wife, arms in the air; sometimes holding her hand, and with a look, saying, *Let's go*.

Without a master's degree for this job, without a manual on how to be the best dad, often without support from anyone, these are the men that hold a family. Not perfect, grumpy at times, short tempered at others, but oh, so crazy in love with those they need to take care of.

All this, with a heart eager to give, to guide, to embrace.

~Manola Secaira

34

SHELDON SWEENEY

Sheldon Sweeney is husband and father who works as a wealth advisor, specializing in retirement planning and planning for families who have children with special needs. Sheldon enjoys open water swimming, disc golf, travelling, and learning how to be a grandparent. Sheldon and his wife live in Maple Valley, Washington.

Striving to be a good father means first, being a good husband. Following the example of St. Joseph, who was extremely attentive to Mary's needs first. Then, as a couple, united in purpose and their faith in God, they moved forward and became parents.

Looking to the Holy Family as role models feels daunting. However, I have found that asking St. Joseph for his intercession through prayer, as a husband and a father is extremely comforting and fruitful.

I have always felt that fatherhood is not only an extension of being in a strong marriage, but also an assignment from God to look after His children. We do the best we can as parents and make a million mistakes. Since my wife and I share the procreative power with God and have children to raise, I think it is important to understand that God has a plan for the lives of our children. As earthly parents, we can have an impact similar to that of St. Joseph with Jesus, serving as an earthly father. And, much like Joseph, we cannot even imagine what God has planned for the lives of our children.

Because I have found myself taking this third-party view of fatherhood, I am able to avoid stress about my children's futures and really enjoy being a father. My favorite part of fatherhood is learning what is exciting for my children and getting involved myself. I like getting excited about baseball, disc golf, Ultimate Frisbee, football, water polo, playing music, dance recitals, and Special Olympics: it's a way for me to be closer to my kids.

My wife Debbie and I have five young adult children and one grandchild as of this writing. We have been married for 34 years. Our first three children were boys, followed by two beautiful girls. (I was far more involved with the boy's activities when they were growing up, as you will notice from the list above.)

My girls came into the world in dramatic fashion. Our oldest daughter Anne was born early due to a severe case of lupus that my wife endured all through her pregnancy. Our doctor at the time recommended an abortion because she said she could not save both lives. I sat at a long boardroom table in the hospital and explained that both lives were of equal value and they needed to find a way to save both. They figured it out.

Our second daughter, Charlotte, was also born early and with Down syndrome. She is now 20 and continues to be the light of our family. One of the benefits of raising a child with special needs and cognitive impairment is that it extends our parenting years beyond that of a typically developing child.

Parenting and fatherhood is best done in communion with other like-minded friends. I appreciate our Catholic church family and could not have been an effective father without the support of parish families. Strong families of faith and strong fathers in our circle of friends helped form and shape our children into the wonderful adults they are.

"Teach us to number our days, that we
may gain a heart of wisdom."

– Psalm 90:12

35

DOUG LAWRENCE

Doug Lawrence has been married to his high school sweetheart, Arlyn, for 40 years; they are the parents of five grown children. They enjoy island living in the Pacific Northwest where Doug works in real estate and enjoys DIY-ing, spending time in his woodworking shop, camping in his rooftop tent, and investing in the lives of his children and 11 grandchildren.

I was brought up in a very loving, faith-filled home, where love was often spoken and put on display in tangible ways. My father, however, was a strict disciplinarian, and when a line was crossed or an expectation was not met, he was very quick and sometimes very harsh in relating his dissatisfaction with a particular circumstance. I, in turn, grew up with a thick hide and a sense that my heavenly Father had the same standards when I failed to meet expectations.

When I became a father and started raising my family, I came to the realization that I was governing my children the same way my father governed his, with a standard and expectation that needed to be met. Sometime in my thirties, I had an epiphany … that God's love for me was unconditional. I came to understand that unlike my father's love, which at times seemed so conditional, my heavenly Father's love was in fact unconditional. My personal revelation was life-changing! This understanding allowed me, perhaps for the first time, to actualize and experience God's real, unconditional love in a tangible and palpable way.

This realization was a huge turning point in the way I parented my own children. If I could not sin my way out of my heavenly Father's perfect love for me, then—*hello!*—my earthly children could not sin their way out my love for them. I am the father of five amazing children and grandfather to eleven (so far). I can say there have been times over the years when my kids have put my thesis to the test. I can also guarantee you that I will get to exercise my truth many more times in my lifetime. It is important—no, it is *critical* that as fathers, grandfathers, uncles, or whatever roles we play, the children in our lives hear in our words and see in our actions our unconditional love for them.

Scripture is full of examples of how we are to live and how we are to love, but learning to love our children selflessly, without judgement, without harsh words, and without anger is truly a huge responsibility. I would even go as far as to say that we *must* learn to love without any expectations in return. After all, is that not how our Creator loves us?

I remember a time when one our kids messed up, as they all inevitably do. As I was preparing for our initial conversation to get the facts, I found myself getting angry and anxious, as I was deeply disappointed by their actions. I then reminded myself of God's love for me and how I was a conduit of that love to my children. The conversation was admittedly difficult, at first, on both sides. However, the emotional damage was limited as I started the conversation with, "I want you to know that whatever you have done, it does not and cannot change my love for you."

As fathers, we must learn to love this way—as God loves us.

36

DIEGO WENDT

Diego Wendt is a commercial pilot (USAF Retired) and the founder of 4US.org, a nonprofit that provides ultrasound machines to pregnancy centers around the world. He lives in Coeur d'Alene, Idaho with his wife, Kim, and their four children.

My wife and I were streaming mind-numbing TV when a late-night knock came at our bedroom door. Our 17-year-old daughter's face slowly appeared, dimly lit with a look of deep concern.

"Hey, Lanie, what's up?" my wife asked as I fumbled for the remote to pause *Downton Abbey.*

"Well, we need to talk," she said, looking over to me as I sat up trying to put on my best "wise father" facial expression.

"Sure," I said. "What's going on?"

"Do you promise you won't get mad?" she asked, eyes darting between Kim and me before settling on me.

My stomach turned, time slowed, and my mind spun into panicky assumptions behind my Ward Cleaver expression: *It must be something big. What's the biggest news it could be? Is she pregnant? No way! She can't be! But what if she is? Is this really happening? I didn't even know she had a boyfriend. Well, isn't this ironic: here we are running a pro-life ministry, and now God is testing me! Relax—we can do this; she won't have to abandon her college and career aspirations. We can help her raise the baby. We'll be the best grandparents ever! We'll …*

"Dad?"

I snapped back into the present. "Of course, we won't get mad."

She took another step in, swallowed, drew a deep breath, and let it out: "Is it okay if I don't apply to the Air Force Academy?"

Kim, a retired Air Force pilot and Academy grad, burst out laughing. Lanie looked confused. My sphincter released its grip on the pillowtop mattress.

I said in my finest "father-knows-best" cadence, "Lanie, what have we always wanted for you?"

"Success."

"No, we've never said that. Try again."

"You want me to be happy."

"No. Life is suffering, and suffering brings meaning to the occasional moments of joy. Come on, what do we want for you?"

"Oh yes … to get to Heaven."

"Right! Can you get to Heaven without going to the Air Force Academy?"

"Yes."

"Then we're good with it."

Lanie's smile exploded across her face as she came bedside to hug Kim who was now crying tears of joy, interrupted by spasms of laughter.

I, on the other hand, sat dumbstruck with so many questions. Had we put too much pressure on her? How had she lost sight of our family motto, which we had repeated almost daily over a decade?

Since that evening, it has been my mission to ensure each one of our four kids actually infuses our very simple family motto into their daily decision making: "Love God, love everybody, get to Heaven." Life has a way of sneaking up on us and muddying our priorities. Lanie's harrowing test that evening reminded me that both she and I needed to set our sights on Heaven and trust God with our circumstances—real or imagined!

37

MIGUEL ROSALES

Miguel Rosales is married to Erika and the father of three sons. He was born in Colima, Mexico and has lived in the USA since he was five, when he moved to Yakima, Washington. His wife states, "He is the leader and patriarch of our family and for his parents and siblings as well. He is not only a loving father and husband but also a caring son and brother." Miguel started E&M Drywall in 2006 and has been in the drywall industry for over 20 years.

Before becoming a father, I never imagined how much I would be willing to do for my three boys.

My wife and I welcomed Adrian, our oldest, to this earth with a lot of love and a lot of nervousness: we were only 19 and 18 years old. Describing us as "unprepared" was an understatement in many people's eyes, but not God's.

I was raised by a very quiet teacher and father. He did not talk much, but he raised us with kindness and showed his love through actions. He worked hard to put food on the table for our family of six, he was always present in the most important moments, and he always demonstrated his affection for us children. He made us feel safe and loved. I could go on and on about this man and how much he taught me, but the point is that I knew I wanted to walk in his shoes and give my children the same love.

Immediately after holding Adrian for the first time, I felt the weight of responsibility for this newborn's well-being: I resolved to make sure he was always fed, always warm and comfortable, and always dressed nicely. Becoming a father gave me a drive I would not otherwise have had at that young stage of life. I embraced the pressure of fatherhood quickly; there was nothing I would not face or do for my precious gift from God.

These days, I feel even more blessed and loved, because after the arrival of two more sons, I feel like I receive from my children what I offer them. It brings me joy to listen to my youngest say his morning prayers before he goes to school or my older boys saying grace before every meal. It brings me peace to receive their warm hugs and know they are grateful for the little we have. A sincere "Thanks, Dad" is a great payment for being a father. The love I have received is incomparable.

I try so hard to never disappoint my boys. They push me to walk as straight as I can so I can be their role model and form three righteous men. When it's time for them to leave our nest, they will be prepared to form their own, and I pray they will remember me as I remember my OWN father.

"A father's job is not to teach his daughter how to be a lady. It's to teach her how a lady should be treated."
- Author Unknown

38

TIM McDANIEL

Tim McDaniel was born in Denver, Colorado, where he grew up skiing, hiking, camping, and biking in the mountains of Colorado. He now lives in Tacoma, Washington with his wife, Megan, of 24 years. They have six wonderful children and together try to continue the love of the outdoors Tim enjoyed as a youth. He is a professional land surveyor and is part owner of a land surveying and engineering company. He loves DIY projects and enjoys many opportunities to practice on their 120-year-old house.

There Is Always Room for One More

I am blessed to be the father of six wonderful, wild children and the husband to the most amazing wife and mother any of us could ask for. We are blessed to have had three children biologically and three children through adoption.

We always knew God was calling us to adoption. He had written it on our hearts. Even before we were married, we always included it while talking about how we envisioned our future. Then, as a newly married couple sitting in our little grass hut in the middle of the Pacific Ocean while serving in the Peace Corps, we prayed for a family. We never knew what the outcome would look like, and it has turned out differently than we first thought, but God has been right there beside us, leading the way the whole time. Through the challenges and heartaches, joys and triumphs, we could not have envisioned a more fulfilling life.

When I look at this crazy crew around me, I often wonder, *How did I get here?* I was as likely to be a hermit living in the mountains as trying to answer the call of shepherding this motley crew to Heaven. The more children we have had, the more I realize that most things in this life are out of our control. The only way forward is with a childlike reliance on God, trusting in His plan. He always answers our prayers with "Yes," "No," or "I have something better for you."

We have a sign hanging in our kitchen that says, "There is always room for one more." This is one of many family mottos we McDaniels have, along with "We love creative messes" and "We strive to be the people God made us to be." But above all, "room for one more" epitomizes what we want our family to be about. We want our kids at home as much and as long as possible to soak up the blessings of a big family. We do not want our home to be isolated and tucked away from the world. We want our kids to enjoy our little domestic church and be prepared to go out into

Train up a child in the way he should go; even when he is old he will not depart from it."

- Proverbs 22:6

the world. We want our kids' friends and classmates at our home to share in the chaos and joy of life. But most importantly, we want all our hearts open to the needs of others so we can save room for people God brings into our lives who need a hand.

St. Thomas Aquinas tells us, "To love is to will the good of the other." Love costs something. The call to kindness and helping others is not always easy, and learning to do this at home before going out to serve the world is key. Without sacrifice for another, there is no love. You can't just want it to happen; it takes some effort with the grace of God behind you to make the sacrifices necessary to love and serve another. Just as God sacrificed animals to

make garments of skin to clothe Adam and Eve out of a deep love for them, we sacrifice our own preferences and conveniences out of a deep love for others..

Love costs some restless nights awake with a sick child. It costs not always getting what we want if it is not what the family needs. It costs not always owning the best things. It costs dings in the walls and dents in the cars. It costs eating grilled cheese and chicken nuggets over and over. However, there is nothing more worth those sacrifices than seeing the joy in a little one's face, their sense of accomplishment when they achieve a goal, or the consolation they feel from our support in tough times. I can think of many other titles I have been called in life, but I cannot think of any other as worth it as that of being called "Dad."

JD FITZ

JD is a retired hospital-based internist who lives adventurously and well with Leigh, his wife of 49 years, in Tacoma Washington. In addition to being a husband to one, he's a dad to three, a father-in-law to three, a papa to five, a brother to another three, and a friend to more than he can remember. He loves outdoor recreation and gardening in mulch. He gets together frequently with friends and family, and enjoys relationships and mentoring. More recently, he has been the lead cheerleader for his wife in the publication of her book, *Art and Soul.* Realizing that the seasons are passing quickly, he is valuing his time with friends and family, trying mightily to not take any of it for granted or too seriously.

Relinquishment

That's what it is about, isn't it? She lives for nine months in the uterus–her life totally dependent on mom's choices. Once she is born, she breathes on her own, but remains dependent on us for food, hygiene, clothing, safety and encouragement. Soon she dresses herself and is off to school. Now we're taxi drivers, behavior managers and short-order cooks. Suddenly, and before we know it, she's off to college, young adulthood, marriage, and her own children. We become cheerleaders and observers, and perhaps if we're lucky, counselors and friends. A short while later we require care ourselves. Life cycles.

Which transition is hardest? I longed to be a dad and I loved parenting, thinking that each stage was the greatest yet. Until, that is, their arc curved away from my expectations for them as they fought, manipulated, danced, and laughed their way through adolescence. Father apparently *didn't* know best and they *weren't* afraid to tell me so. My self-confidence met their reality.

What do you do then? This inflection point is where I had to decide whether to "take my stand" and fight or to relinquish what I considered to be my "God-given" sense of having to be in control and then make a strategic and progressive retreat. I reluctantly (or more honestly), I was forced, to release, rethink, recalibrate, and most of all, relinquish this area of control. I discovered that certain changes were inevitable: seasons, tides, and adolescence.

It's bittersweet, right? The good news is that it gets easier. As I have relinquished my need for choosing life paths for these wonderful people, they have chosen to be my friends. I now live in the wonderful world of "fathering without parenting" and have very few responsibilities left to give up.

But will I ever relinquish the sense that I could have done better? I'm working on it.

40

CHRISTOPHER KIMBALL

Christopher Kimball is a Certified Financial Planner practitioner who holds the professional designations of Accredited Estate Planner, Certified in Long-Term Care, and Chartered Mutual Fund Counselor. He received his Bachelor of Arts degree from the University of Washington, a Master of Science in Financial Services degree from the American College, and Master of Divinity, Masters of Biblical Studies, and Doctor of Ministry degrees from Covenant Bible Seminary. In addition to his Financial Planning Office, Chris also teaches apologetics at Covenant Bible Seminary. He lives with his wife and two miniature Dachshunds in University Place, Washington. Their two sons and daughters-in-law live in nearby Tacoma.

Lying in bed, I stared at the ceiling…and waited. I waited for the sound I had heard so many times before over the past three years. The sound I dreaded. But there it was again—a wail followed by sobs of disappointment. The pregnancy test was negative.

My wife and I had always wanted children. Even before we met, each of us looked forward to the day we could marry and raise a family. We'd done all we could. We'd prayed and cried and sought advice, but still no children.

Then, one glorious day, our prayers were answered. Vicki was pregnant!

The day David was born we experienced more joy than we thought possible. Twenty-two months later our second son, Donald, joined his brother, and the joy multiplied. I had no idea the love I felt for my children would be so deep.

Since before they were born, I've prayed daily for my sons. A wise friend advised me to pray for their future wives, too.

As they grew, Vicki and I decided she would leave her profession in order to homeschool. Fortunately, my schedule allowed me to spend one day during the week at home while Vicki transitioned from full-time work to part-time, and finally to full-time, homeschooling duties. It was a financial sacrifice, but when it comes to investments, there's nothing better than devoting your time and treasure to your family.

Originally, I was tasked with teaching physical education and science. However, when Vicki discovered my PE lessons consisted of me sitting on a chair watching the boys do jumping jacks, and after my instruction of rocket theory resulted in an exploding plastic pop bottle (to the consternation of our neighbors), I was relieved of my teaching duties. It was decided I was better at

showing them how to mow the lawn, fix things, and learn woodworking.

Our family did a lot of activities together, from daily devotionals to playing McCitement. McCitement was the particularly sophisticated game we invented ourselves—throwing foam balls at each other until exhaustion prevailed! As a family, we also prepared and performed music or humorous readings for our church and my local Rotary club.

We loved spending time with our sons: helping them buy their first cars, giving advice about first dates, supporting them in their first drama production, and when needed, just listening. Their willingness to open their hearts and share their deepest thoughts with Vicki and me was, and is, a true blessing.

PART 6

Passing the Baton

From generation to generation—
we always need our dads!

My dad doesn't know what day it is.
He doesn't remember what he had for lunch.
And sometimes his sweater is inside out.
But none of that matters…
His fatherly love is fully intact, maybe even more than ever before.
When I enter the room his eyes light up.
His gratitude and love flow out of his heart; he listens and is fully present.

Fathers have the weight of the world on their shoulders.
They are providing and protecting and strong.
But they also are the soft place to land and the shoulder to cry on.

When I was 27 my husband Jon Syren died of cancer.
As I exited the airplane with my two little children,
having flown back home after the funeral,
there was my dad.

I collapsed into his arms.
He held me and my babies as we sobbed.
He was the soft place to land.

Jon was such a good father, a beautiful soul who died peacefully.
The biggest hurdle for him being leaving me and our two babies.
He swore he would take care of us from Heaven and he has.
And he brought my husband Jack and me together.

When I married Jack, he adopted my two little ones.
Since then we have had seven more children.
Jack is such a good father and loves each of our nine fully.

Judge Larkin spoke to my children at the adoption hearing.
"You have two daddies…one in Heaven and one on Earth."
All nine of my kids know this inherently.
It's as if there's a father tag team happening all the time.

I have been blessed with three examples of amazing fathers.
I deeply know the veil is very thin between Heaven and Earth.
Someday my dad will pass on.
He will join in the symphony of fatherly love and guidance from above.

Fathers are important, grandfathers are important, stepfathers are important.
You provide, protect, and are a soft place to land.
Keep going—
from generation to generation.

~Angela Connelly

JON McDANIEL

Jon McDaniel is a retired land surveyor and part owner of a surveying and engineering company in Denver, Colorado. He has been married to his wife, Patty, for 50 years. The couple has four children, 11 grandchildren, and one-great granddaughter (so far). Jon believes that "stories stitch families together."

"Speak to them of the great mercy of God. Sometimes people are helped by your telling of your lamentable past."

~St. Francis Xavier

When our children were young, my wife Patty and I made it a family tradition to read stories to them at each bedtime. One night, after Patty had first read one or two of their favorites—*Miss Suzy, Socks For Supper, Wacky Wednesday, Love You Forever*, et cetera—I switched things up by telling them a personal story of my youth from what became a series called "Dumb Things I Did When I Was A Kid."

The children loved it. From then on, the highlight of every bedtime became the request, "Daddy, tell us some dumb things you did when you were a kid."

Since I wised up somewhat as I grew older, I soon ran out of "dumb" stories and added other adventures of my youthful years growing up in the small town of Sturgis, South Dakota.

The kids' favorite was "The Gumball Machine." When I was nine or 10 and in possession of a nickel, I walked the mile or so down Main Street to the Ben Franklin five-and-dime store. Inside, on a shiny metal stand, was the gumball machine, a glass globe full of multicolored gumballs. I placed my nickel in the slot, rotated the lever that dropped the coin into a tray, and expected to see a shiny gumball drop out from the globe into the dispensing tray. It didn't! I was mad and stuck my finger up in the dispenser to try to jiggle my gumball out. But the lever slipped and clamped shut on my finger. I was stuck! I began to wail in pain, fear, and embarrassment.

The store manager ran to the scene, assessed my dilemma, and promptly departed.

He returned with tools to disassemble the gumball machine and free my finger. He succeeded, but he failed to account for what would happen when he removed the glass ball. Hundreds of gumballs cascaded to the floor, bouncing and ricocheting and rolling down the aisles throughout the entire store, much to the chagrin of the now-angry manager.

Terrified of retribution, I ran from the store and, I'm sure, all the way home too. Only later did I realize I had failed to grab a gumball on the way out.

Our four children never tired of hearing these stories, and later, our 11 grandkids also enjoyed hearing about their papa being a kid long ago. Children don't usually think of their parents as having once been children themselves. I think we become more relatable, more approachable, when they see how we made mistakes when we were young, learned from them, were forgiven, and later reflect on them from a humorous point of view.

I feel l am a better father and grandfather because of my storytelling. It has created a warm, cozy atmosphere each bedtime for the kids and fond memories for them and me. They are a way for me to imitate Jesus's love for little ones: "Let the little children come to me, and do not stop them; for it is to such as these that the kingdom of heaven belongs" (Matthew 19:14).

Feel free to borrow "The Gumball Machine" for your own kids and grandkids. Next time, I'll tell you about the "Creepy Game"—it involves a dark basement and a flashlight!

"Give me a sense of humor, Lord,
and something to laugh about."

– St. Thomas More

MIKE PERRY

Kevin Perry was born and raised in Waterford, Connecticut, and served in the Navy for four years. He owned KM Perry Trucking, Inc. for 35 years and is currently a corporate auditor for Quality Transport, Inc. Kevin and his wife, Laura, perfected the art of paint balling as they raised their two sons in Tacoma, Washington.

In my teen years, my relationship with my father was often strained. He was a self-employed entrepreneur, and his work life included long days that went late into the night. My mother, my three siblings, and I didn't see him much. Also, a seesaw of business successes and failures affected his temper—and not in a good way. I see this now in retrospect with understanding and compassion. However, at the age of fifteen, my heart was hardened against him.

One day, sitting in the living room, my father attempted to engage me, his surly 15-year-old son, in a conversation. I avoided his gaze and looked out the window to see an old man on the sidewalk, hunched over and walking with a cane. We both watched this man as he slowly plodded on, both of us relieved to turn our focus to a third party.

As we watched, the man's foot struck an irregularity in the sidewalk, and he toppled to the ground. My father immediately jumped out of his chair and ran out the door to assist the man.

As for me, I remained in my chair. *Oh, he'll get up*, I thought.

I was eventually roused from my seat by a twinge of guilt, and I sauntered out the door to see what was happening. When I reached the sidewalk, I noticed my father kneeling over the man and gently comforting him, cradling his head in his hand to protect it from the concrete.

I stood and looked at the two for some time. This was a side of my father I had never seen, and watching him worked two powerful changes within me. First, I experienced a sense of shame at my indifference to the old man's suffering. Next, I realized that my heart had softened toward my father. I now understood that he was much better than me.

This image of my father remains with me even now, though it is close to twenty years since he passed. In that moment years ago, I was pleased to be his son. I knew he was a good man. This earthly father gave me a heart that could cry out to God. What a blessing to have this example in my memory so that I can, without hesitation, cry, "Abba, Father!" to my heavenly Father!

God is still writing your story.
Quit trying to steal the pen.
Trust the Author.

43

BRENT BECKSTEAD

Brent Beckstead was born in Tacoma, Washington and spent nearly 30 years teaching there, which he enjoyed immensely. Since he was young, he has loved to travel alone as well as with friends and family. He travelled throughout the world with his wife and son to all seven continents. Brent likes to quote, "God gives us life through family from the time we're born to the time we pass." Brent also has a passion for discussing politics over coffee, reading, and hiking with his son. You can find him nearly every morning at the Proctor Starbucks.

In our travels to lands near and far, my family has always helped each other on the trails. We offer a hand to each other to balance, pull, brace, and assist. It began when my wife and I would hold hands on walks and hikes, but then our son Jordan was born. I enjoy walking and hiking with both my wife and our son, but Jordan holds a special, adventurous place in my heart.

When Jordan was a small child, I carried him in a backpack contraption on afternoon walks in the neighborhood. Sometimes I'd reach up to hold his hands as we traversed puddles, creeks, and difficult patches. As he grew old enough to walk, he started forging ahead, stomping through those same puddles I had tried to avoid while he was on my back. But he still held on to me: he would reach for my hand in challenging spots, or I would offer it. Sometimes, we would hold hands the entire walk, even while strolling through the neighborhood grocery store or along the paved pathways along the waterfront.

For the next few years, I'd reach for his hand to help him along or just as an occasional balance. As he grew older, Jordan needed me less and less. We began to share

our hands with each other to go over or under fallen trees and roots, to balance through creeks and over boulders, and to negotiate our way around stumps and other obstacles.

Now, as an adult, it is not that unusual for Jordan to call me and warn me of impending weather conditions, particularly heavy rains, in the forthcoming days. So I wasn't surprised when one evening, a few days after the start of winter, I received a call warning me of ice covering the area the next morning. Jordan ordered me to stay home and to not go out of the house for my usual morning coffee. He promised to bring coffee to me at 9:00 a.m.

Well, the next morning, I woke up at about 5:15 and automatically washed, dressed, and headed to coffee. Even after the warning from my son, I was determined to meet with my friends. Very carefully, I made it to the car and on to Starbucks. The roads and sidewalks were slick with ice as he had warned. I had my usual coffee and morning discussion. However, being a little scared Jordan might catch me going out on the terrible icy streets, I decided to head out early and get home before he arrived (yes, I'm 70 years old and worried if I'll get in trouble with my son).

With plenty of time to spare, I arrived home at 8:00 a.m. and began my slow, treacherous trek up to the house. With an excess of caution, I walked up on the lawn instead of the icy sloped path. All went as planned until I was a few steps from the door. Now, I needed to step carefully onto the walkway before the stairs. It was only a few feet.

I took the first step onto the ice-covered concrete path and said to myself, "I've got this"—as I slipped and faceplanted in the garden. With a bloody nose, a scratched-up face, and a pain in my side, I crawled to the stairs and pulled myself up on the railings. Once inside, I headed to the bathroom to clean up. I then moved to the living room to quietly listen to music.

Shortly thereafter, Jordan showed up, took one look at me, and said, "I told you not to go out." Reaching down to me, he said, "Here Dad, take my hand. I'll help you up."

I was choked up. It had come full circle.

A good father is one of the most unsung, unpraised, unnoticed, and yet one of the most valuable assets in our society.

- Billy Graham

44

LADD WOLFE

Ladd Wolfe, a teacher, runner, and outdoor adventurer, grew up on a small farm in Oregon. As one of seven children, he had the blessing of parents who knew how to draw the circle of family widely to include not only guests for Sunday dinners, but most importantly, his sisters adopted from Korea. He and his wife, Elizabeth, have raised their three girls for over 30 years, exploring all that the Pacific Northwest has to offer.

Hold You

"Hold you."

I knew what she meant. She meant, "I want *you* to hold *me*." But as a father, looking down at my little girl, with her arms stretched up toward me, I thought, *'Hold you' seems somehow more fitting.*

It isn't so much what we need or want for ourselves, but rather how we can hold each other. Hold each other when a day has been difficult, hold each other in quick squeezes of love when seeing each other again, and holding each other up to the Father in prayer each day.

As my girls grow older, parenting looks and feels different. I wouldn't be honest if I didn't say I miss those days of my little girls scrambling up in my lap for an evening read-aloud and of course, some giggling and tickling. As they've grown older, I have felt my chest swell with pride at their accomplishments, and I have cringed when I've heard them speak on some topics. But somewhere along the line, I have learned to step back and realize I'm not "in the know" about all of God's plans for my children. I must daily set aside my human impulse to solve things on my own. I pray, "Lord, I can't see through the muck I'm experiencing right now, but I lean on You, I trust You know what's at the end, and You've got this, not me. God, show me today what it is You've been up to and how I can serve and be a part of those good things."

In a quote attributed to Mother Teresa, it's said:

"Children are like kites; you will teach them to fly but they will not take your flight-path. You will teach them to dream, but they will not dream your dream. You will teach them to live, but they will not live your life. Yet in every flight, in every dream, and in every life, the mark of the teachings that have been received will always remain."

And so again, I pray, "Father, in the name of Jesus, I pray your Holy Spirit draws my children to You. Wherever they go, whatever they do, surround them with Spirit-filled Jesus people who know Your love and Your power. Father, I thank You that You are smarter than any human. Let them see Your undeniable love for them each day. I call them into the kingdom in Jesus's name."

Let each day be a day when we rely less on ourselves as fathers and look up to the Lord God, our Father, and with raised hands say, "Hold You."

45

BEN CRAMER

Ben Cramer is a small business owner in Tacoma, Washington. He and his wife Gail were married for 48 years, enjoying home renovations and master gardening, until her passing. Ben receives great joy from his two adult children and three grandchildren, attending all of their sports and celebrations as their biggest fan. In his grief, Ben says, "Writing saved me."

Fatherhood

Life, no matter how you cut it, is a matter of choices. From the time we are children choosing one toy over another, we make choices, and those choices determine the course of our lives.

I was raised by a caring mother and an angry father. Neither had much to do with me, though: I was the last child and much younger than my siblings. Regardless of how you were raised, we still choose not to let our past dictate how you will live your future life. From the time we begin to understand our surroundings we form opinions. I can remember early in life, I noticed things about my parents, particularly my father, that were not to my liking. For example, my father never spent time with me. There were no stereotypical playful interactions like playing catch or building a fort. And neither my mom or dad ever attended my school functions or sporting events. There seemed to be a disconnect between us, which I did not (could not) understand.

My parents made choices that served them. My father drank in excess and was depressed a good deal of the time, which prevented him from being interested in me. As I grew older, I saw how other families interacted with one another. I decided in my mid-teens that I would not pattern myself after my family, but rather learn from others' examples.

I met my wife to be when I returned from the military. We were married at 21. She, too, came from a dysfunctional household. We spent many of our courting hours talking about how we would not be poor examples to our children and began to dream about a family made with love and intention. We welcomed our own children into the world, and as they grew older, we emphasized to them the importance of making right choices. We shared our own experiences of growing up and how we wanted things to be different for them. We tried to lead by example, and for the most part, we were successful in that approach. One of our shortfalls was neglecting to instill in them a religious foundation. I have always had some guilt

about this, but they have each become their own people and have made their own good choices.

My children are good citizens, and I tell anyone who will listen that if my children were not my children, I would want them as my friends.

Now as a grandpa, and friend to my adult children, I am convinced and consoled that our past is merely a place of reference and not residence.

46

FRANK COUSENS

Francis Cousens, devoted spouse of Sandra and proud father of Elizabeth, retired from his role as a professor at the University of Puget Sound in Tacoma, Washington. His previous experience included military service as a linguist and teaching at the University of California.

My wife and I raised one child: our daughter, Elizabeth, who has been the light of our lives from the beginning. I am flooded with happy memories when I think about her growing up and confronting the challenges of life at every stage, from the predictable tensions of school and university to the gratifying pleasures of professional achievement.

After my own study at the U. S. Army Language School as part of my military service and the completion of graduate work at USC, I discovered the sheer joy of teaching college- and university-level students. Always in love with learning for its own sake, I took great delight in sharing my enthusiasm for literature and philosophy with eager young people. I received immense satisfaction from the passion ignited in individuals by exposure to great ideas couched in memorable language.

When Elizabeth started on her own quest for knowledge, as her proud father, I enjoyed the intermingling of my two worlds, fatherhood and mentorship. I discovered that parenting and teaching could be two sides of the same coin. Elizabeth proved to be an incredibly energetic and capable student who far exceeded my expectations for the ideal learner who could forge her own path.

Ironically, she went on to fulfill one of my deepest and fondest personal dreams: residence at and degrees from Oxford University in England. For me, her experiences there were a vicarious joy of reclaimed aspirations.

When Elizabeth revealed that she was in the running for a Rhodes Scholarship, I felt a revival of old enthusiasms that powered my spirit. She had surpassed my limited ambitions and, as a Rhodes Scholar, earned two advanced degrees from Oxford University. The "dreaming spires" of that magical setting became her intellectual home for three years.

Deeply committed to doing work to benefit the world, she now heads an organization with close ties to the United Nations. During her international travels, she had the good fortune to find in Ethiopia a baby boy available for adoption: he is now a teenager readying himself for high school as Elizabeth proudly looks on, much as her mother and I did with her.

These kinds of parental blessings are a delight to tally when they sweeten the mind and spirit with loving memories, along with hope and anticipation for the future.

47

DANIEL FREDERICK

Daniel Frederick lives in Poulsbo, Washington and is the husband of Hannah and father to Elliot and Evangeline. He works as the executive director of The Coffee Oasis. In 1997, Daniel's family started The Coffee Oasis with a passion to reach hurting youth in their community. Twenty-four years later, The Coffee Oasis continues to offer hope, housing, and resources to young people throughout Kitsap and Pierce County. Daniel's early years were spent doing odd jobs around The Coffee Oasis and he now has the privilege of leading an amazing team with the goal of restoring community through compassionate youth programs and coffee businesses. *www.thecoffeeoasis.com*

"Need you, Dad."

These are the words my son, Elliot, uses to get my attention. He wasn't given the words in this order; his heart put together "need you" and "Dad" and discovered the way the world was made to work. Psychologist Curt Thompson writes, "Every baby comes into the world looking for someone who is looking for him or her … We long to be known forever, ever more deeply and joyfully. We long for that state of confident expectancy with every footfall that lands on life's pavement."

My dad had a complicated relationship with his father, Roland Frederick. Roland was a respected pastor, and to this day, I am told stories of ways he helped people find God. At home, however, Roland was quick to anger and a harsh disciplinarian. My dad rarely shared about his childhood, but one memory continued to surface throughout the years. I don't know the context, only Roland's words that followed my dad into adulthood: "You will never amount to anything." This remark resounded throughout my dad's life.

My dad would go on to be a father to many. I have three siblings—two biological and one adopted. And because of the way he responded to the cry of "need you" for thousands of young people, he holds the honored role of father for many more. In 1997, my parents started a nonprofit called The Coffee Oasis. The mission was simply to "bring the hope of Christ to the pain on the streets." The Coffee Oasis has brought hope to 50,000 homeless and hurting young people. The Coffee Oasis meets many of the needs traditionally met by a mother and father. When a young person walks through the door, their first words call to mind the request of my son: "I need a job" or "I need a place to stay."

I'm reminded of a 14-year-old girl who was brought to our shelter in Tacoma. A Cadillac with tinted windows ousted her on our doorstep. It took a moment for her to unload her few belongings, held together in plastic grocery bags. When the car pulled away, a shelter volunteer asked who

was in the car—sometimes it is a teacher or social worker.

"That was my dad," the girl said.

Sometimes, I like to imagine a very different story for this 14-year-old child. I can hear a quiet voice from the back seat of the Cadillac speaking what is in the heart of every child. "*Need you, Dad.*" And I see her dad's heart breaking and made whole again the moment those words are spoken and her world being made right in the assurance of a father's love.

We are told in Paul's letter to the church of Rome that the Holy Spirit gives us these words to pray, "Abba, Father" (see Romans 8:15). If you are hurting and have forgotten how to speak to God, the role of the Holy Spirit is to lead you back to the Father's love. Healing begins with the Spirit restoring in our hearts the child's cry, "*Need you, Dad.*" I have often reflected on the way God transformed the pain of my dad's childhood into a legacy of meeting the needs of hurting young people who find their way to The Coffee Oasis. My dad was able to be a father to many because he learned the Spirit's cry. And gradually, God's love spoke with more authority than the harsh words of his father, "You'll never amount to anything." There

was nothing he needed to amount to when his belonging and identity were found in being a child of God.

I now walk in that legacy of loving authority. As the Executive Director of The Coffee Oasis and a new father, I'm learning to live in the security of God's love and from that place of belonging respond to the request of my son and thousands of youths who enter the doors of The Coffee Oasis each year saying, "*Need you, Dad.*"

48

FR. JOSEPH SELINGER, O.P.

Father Joseph Selinger, O.P., was born and raised in Vancouver, Canada and ordained as a Dominican Friar in 2022. He serves as a teacher in Portland, Oregon where he shares his love of God, the rosary, and Saint Joseph and spiritual fatherhood.

In our province, we Dominican Monks have the optional custom of taking a religious name when we are invested with the Dominican habit as novices. The Provincial said to me, "In the world, you were known as Aaron, but in the order, you will be known as Brother Joseph."

I picked the name Joseph for two reasons. First, Joseph is my father's confirmation name, and I wanted to honor my father, by whose insistence I was baptized and began my Christian life. Second, I wanted a constant reminder that, as a priest, my vocation is to be a spiritual father. Later, I unearthed a third reason: I had forgotten at the time that Saint Joseph is also the patron saint of Canada, and I was born and raised in Vancouver, Canada. I only came to the United States to live when I entered the Dominican Order in 2014.

Saint Joseph is a spiritual father who inspires all fathers today, whether they are biological or spiritual. Saint Joseph gave himself generously to his foster child Jesus and Mary his wife. He worked diligently for his family with a quiet, dignified humility. He was a man of sacrifice and offered himself in obedience to God's plan, which was manifested to him by an angel.

Moreover, Saint Joseph is a great example of chastity. He respected the perpetual virginity of the Blessed Virgin Mary and gave himself completely to God in the profound spiritual union of charity, that friendship which makes God a second-self to us. He had the fortitude to not be moved from the sorrow caused by the sacrifice of pleasures and immediate gratification. In other words, Saint Joseph was not soft, but was fortified with manliness born of an inner strength that can only come from God.

We therefore ought to praise Joseph for his natural and supernatural virtues. He is a model for us—a model who should provide the measure of our own natural fatherhood and masculinity. He is also a model for women, since he possesses all those virtues that enable an excellent Christian life.

May the Lord bless us as we all strive to live a virtuous life like Saint Joseph!

PART 7

Spiritual Leadership

In my life, I have had both an earthly father and many spiritual ones, but none so great as God.

For most of my life, I considered myself a "daddy's girl." The kinship with my father was founded closely in the way we both approached faith and people. I often quoted him and, before I was married, I prayed for a husband "like" him.

Something happened over those first few decades that shaped the next several too. Seemingly subtle, and certainly surprising; I realized had *learned* to trust, believe, and turn to my dad first, in place of God.

It is tempting to justify this and even to encourage such intimacy because fathers are often a conduit for faith in God. Our dads are tangible and many times they can mirror our Father in Heaven's love. Yet, earthly fathers are first and foremost human: flawed, fallible, and fragile. They can magnify attributes of God but are not God.

The role strain for men is tremendous: all at once they are boys, sons, brothers, workers, friends, boyfriends, priests, teachers, husbands, and fathers. The hopeful truth is found in that we are MORE than the sum of our parts (roles and choices) and, while we may want to ignore or forget our past, the days and years before this moment are always part of what makes us whole: complete, healed, and revealed.

Just as looking at only the corner of a painting, what we can actually "see," might only invite confusion or disappointment. But if we can just adjust our perspective— take a few steps back, allowing for our gaze to behold the picture in its frame—we are more likely to glimpse the Master's signature strokes and possibly even name the Artist.

Although there is always a temptation to despair at any given chapter or plot twist in our life story, I believe that the masterpiece of our lives is not complete until we breathe our last breath. Faith frees me to focus on the fact that every brush stroke wielded by our Father in Heaven is broad, full of love, redemption, grace and mercy.

As an adult, my dad made choices that forever altered the course of his life. His actions were ultimately a catalyst for repairing my impaired, severely limited, perception of God the Father, allowing God to be my Father. This reorienting was not gentle or immediately peaceful; in fact it might best be described as catastrophic. The tears, prayers, conversations, shock, fear and faith that followed proved to be integral tools for breaking free my feet: 45 years cemented in my identity as daughter in my earthly family, and safely moving me onto the only trustworthy and lasting foundation of my life: the Rock Eternal. I truly learned, "And we know that God causes all things to work together for good to those who love God, to those who are called according to *His* purpose" (Romans 8:28)

There was one night when I cried out in prayer lamenting my crushing loneliness, unleashing torrents of sadness in a flood of tears. When I caught my breath, He whispered—tenderly, patiently, lovingly— my name. He reminded and restored my heart recalling every instance where He had been, and still was my Father. The lie that I was alone was silenced and my anchor was firmly set.

This book is a collection of stories of fathers from all walks of life, all of whom desire to be the best representation of their heavenly Father they can be on this earth. Some came from homes where this kind of fatherhood was authentically modeled for them. Others did not, and have had to learn these skills and principles directly from the Father, and leaning on other mentors and influences. Either way, God's grace is with them, and is on you as well.

Fatherhood on Earth looks very different for every person—not just how someone experiences it, but also in how they live it or long for it. At the core of every human person, we are hardwired for connection and meaning. So, in how you lead, whether it be your children, your church, your department at work, or elsewhere, fatherhood is manifested in these ways. Authentic fatherhood is the acknowledgment of God's love, strength, and provision that sets us free to love and be loved.

~Megan McDaniel

"A ship in a harbor is safe, but that's not what ships are built for."
- John A. Shedd

In our society, we ask our men, especially, to hold it all together—
to be in charge, to lead, to have all the answers. We expect a lot
and many times it may seem or feel impossible. It is impossible.
On our own strength and wisdom alone, we will fail. The solution
is gratitude and the acceptance of our status as a child—God's
child. We are the creatures, not the Creator. These truths serve as
a compass. As we are freed to allow God to be God—to be the
One in charge—in faith, we can pull in the anchors and set sail.

49

CHARLES GOODWIN

Charlie Goodwin has been married to his wife, Colleen, for five years and is the father of two daughters, Ione and Quinn. They live on a small farm in Northern California. Charlie is a graduate of Thomas Aquinas College and works in development at Ignatius Press.

A Reflection on Fatherhood

It's 6:30 in the morning. I make a cup of espresso for my wife to sip as she teaches second graders online in the other room. I walk to the barn in my bathrobe, split some fresh wood, and stoke the embers of the fire to warm the house for the day. It takes a few minutes to feed the flame and blow the embers back to life. I pour myself a cup of coffee, sit down, and look forward excitedly to a few moments of prayer, reading, writing, and general quiet and contemplation…then I hear a baby cry. The girls are awake. Now my day really begins!

Before marrying, I spent seven years in a monastery, living a life of prayer, study, and silence. The daily routine was designed to form spiritual fathers. Little did I know that God would call me from that place into marriage and physical fatherhood. Turns out there is a lot of crossover.

I no longer wake before dawn to sing the Psalms in a choir and greet the day, but I do rise early to watch my daughters, ages one and three, while my wife works her part-time teaching job.

I don't eat in silence in the refectory while listening to a table reading, but sometimes I manage to call the Lord to mind as I make breakfast for the girls while trying to keep them (and the kitchen) clean.

I don't wash the hands of the priest as I serve at mass, but I do wash up my daughters after I fail to keep breakfast a clean affair.

I don't spend hours studying philosophy and theology, but I often encounter an unexpected and pristine wisdom in an offhand comment from my three year old: "Look at the moon! It's a ball!"

I no longer live under a vow of poverty, but my funds have a habit of dissipating into causes founded in fatherhood—mortgage, groceries, Target—and car repairs always appear when the savings account starts to get cocky.

I no longer live under a vow of chastity, but daughters have a way of honing the need for inner integrity and strength in a man's soul. I belong totally to my girls.

I no longer live under a vow of obedience, but my time is certainly not my own. I have new superiors now.

I used to end my days with a peaceful holy hour, often dozing off in the arms of the Lord. Now, I end my days with my daughters dozing off in mine.

In 1964, Father Karol Wojtyla wrote a play called *The Radiation of Fatherhood*. The play begins with the premise that all light shines forth from God the Father and we participate in that light.

Whether a priest or a dad, we have to choose to allow the radiance of the Father to shine through us onto our children. Father Wojtyla says that mothers share in this radiation, for there are no fathers without mothers. In the end, he observes that the very order of reality is embraced by this radiation of fatherhood. We all share, or choose not to share, in the creative love of the Father, a love that brings forth new life.

As a father, I set my sights on doing all that I can to allow the light of the Father to shine through me onto my family and into the world. And I believe that this can happen at any moment and in any circumstance—in the silence of the monastery or in the joyful riot of the home.

"Give away love like you're made of the stuff;
we're rehearsing to spend eternity together."

– Bob Goff

50

MICHAEL O'ROURKE

Michael O'Rourke grew up in Fresno, California and attended the University of Notre Dame, where he met his wife, Maria. Together, they have 10 children and five grandchildren. He is passionate about his Catholic faith, fatherhood, and helping parents fulfill God's command: "You shall diligently teach your children the faith at home, whether you are busy or at rest." (Deuteronomy 6:7) Michael founded FamilyConquest to help parents captivate their children's imagination through viral videos on magic, miracles, sports, science, nature, and humor as a backdrop to unveil the truths of the Catholic faith. *www.FamilyConquest.org*

I'm blessed to have 10 children between the ages of six and 27. I didn't start out wanting to have a large family. I came from a family of four, my wife came from a family of eight, and when we talked about how many kids we wanted to have, I remember saying I wanted a "big family like mine." My wife, Maria? She was smartly silent. She wanted to be open to *far* more children, and she knew that with time, I'd come around.

So, what was it like being open to even the first child? *I was scared to death.* How was I going to be able to provide for another person, an immortal soul? I didn't even have a job at the time!

But then, my father-in-law pulled me aside and said that *his* father-in-law had told him every child comes with a loaf of bread under their arm.

"What does that mean?" I asked him.

"When God gives you a child, He gives

you the means to provide for that child."

I remember thinking how I had just graduated from college, completed a year of volunteer work, and had $20,000 worth of loans, while my father-in-law was a successful physician. How were our situations even remotely similar? But he reminded me he was still in medical school acquiring debt when he started his family, and they went on to have eight children. God provided for them, and He would provide for me.

So, while I was scared to death, with each child there indeed came a loaf of bread. You could basically plot my income going up with each child, though it usually went up *after* we found out we were pregnant. I would get a promotion, something else would come through, or sometimes family members would just help us out. We were taken care of over and over.

To be honest, though, it wasn't until about my fifth child I started to realize what was going on, and maybe I *could*

trust the Lord. It was like I could almost hear Him saying, "Have you finally figured it out, Michael? Yes, I will take care of you."

Another interesting thing about large families: my parents only had four sons, but they used to get our names wrong all the time. I promised myself I was never going to do that, regardless of how many kids I had.

So people ask me now if I remember the names of all my kids, and the answer is, "Of course! Do you have 10 friends? Do you remember all their names? Of course, you do!" However, when I'm angry or upset about something and I want to call out one of my kids, that's the moment when the wrong child's name comes out. It's almost like my brain is in overdrive and I can't get out the right name … so sometimes, I do *exactly* what my parents did after all!

The most surprising thing about a big family is how there are almost two halves of the group: the older kids and the younger kids. The older kids were basically our guinea pigs; we were learning to parent and we did a lot of things wrong with them. At times I've had discussions with our Lord about why He let me, as a new, incompetent parent, even be a father in the first place.

My older kids have had to pay that price. There were things we freaked out about that we now realize weren't a big deal, and there were also things that we missed that *were* important. Thankfully, we have parented the younger part of the family better. We're better at picking up on the important things and letting the nonessentials go.

I was recently sharing with my wife's aunt how we've avoided our past mistakes with the younger half of the family, and she looked at me and laughed.

"Great!" she said. "With the younger children, you can do new things wrong!"

And she has a point. We're going to do new things wrong. It was pride that made me think I would eventually get everything right. But even though I'm going to get new things wrong, there are also some old things I'm going to do right—and that's a real blessing.

It's an adventure to have a large family. God speaks through my children. I've had to be humble and learn from them, learn from my mistakes, and get back up again. I hope my older children can see some of the ways we parent better now, even though they didn't get that better treatment, and implement those things in their own families.

51

AIRES PATULOT

Aires Patulot is a Catholic speaker, author, musician, and campus minister at Bellarmine High School in Tacoma, Washington. A father of four boys, he is committed to empowering youth and families to rise to God's great calling for each person. He can be heard on the Fatherhood Arise Podcast and his work is published in US Catholic, LTP, and other publications. Visit his website *www.calledtorise.org* or follow him on social media: @calledtorise.

My family is not the "get-to-Mass-early" type. But it was the children's Mass for Christmas Eve and we knew it would be a packed house. We arrived relatively early, at least by our standards. My wife and I, along with our (at the time) three young boys squeezed into the front pew and excitedly chatted away: the long-awaited Christmas activities were now upon us.

During the homily, our pastor asked the kids what they wanted to pray for during this Christmas season. Eager hands raised all around us as children volunteered to share. The good priest walked around with a wireless mic, allowing them to share their heartfelt prayers.

"For the homeless!"

"For the baby in my mommy's tummy!"

At that point, our eight-year-old, Blaise, whispered that he wanted to volunteer.

"What will you pray for?" I asked him.

"World peace," he replied.

A fine answer, I thought to myself, as I envisioned the heavens parting and angels singing "Glory to God in the highest" as world peace descended from on high. His hand shot into the air and Father Bill presented the mic to Blaise.

After the briefest of pauses, my dear, sweet boy declared in his loudest voice, *"Marshawn Lynch!"*

The Seattle Seahawks were in the playoffs and had recently re-signed popular running back Marshawn Lynch. The church erupted in laughter, and mercifully, Father Bill responded, "I think all of us are praying for him!" Grinning wide, my son sat happily in the pew until the end of Mass. Meanwhile, my wife and I squirmed in our seats, exchanging embarrassed glances. Despite all that, I admit it was hilarious.

We aren't a huge football family. Blaise, to my knowledge, is not a giant Lynch fan. His prayer didn't bring about world peace, but it did bring a bit of laughter to our hearts and helped us appreciate the uniqueness of each of our children.

While I wish I could report this moment was an aberration, it's more commonplace than I would like. Going to Mass is chaotic. As we jump into the minivan, the boys are often fighting about something trivial. After we sit down, someone always wants to get back up to get a drink of water or go to the bathroom. My wife and I sit in between each child to ensure maximum supervision and separation from potential slaps and bumps. It's become more hectic as we've added another little boy to the mix.

Even with all this, we make it a priority to attend and participate each Sunday. I try to remind the boys that Jesus is there with us in the Eucharist. We encourage them to offer forgiveness during the sign of peace. After communion, I always ask them to say a prayer for me and assure them I am praying for them. Grace abounds when we gather as the body of Christ. Even when there are surprises, I am grateful we can experience them together.

But next time, no microphones.

52

MILES MUSICK

Miles Musick is a devoted father of six. He and his wife are the founders of YWAM New Beginnings Homes in Puyallup, Washington. For 40 years, their ministry has provided a home and family setting for pregnant women in need.

Papa to 600

God has gifted me eyes to see ways to encourage my children, allowing me to observe the smallest opportunities, such as holding the door for someone or carrying their bag. I would call it my father's heart style: to lift a downcast chin and show love. Put simply, I'm a papa.

With my children, I aim to make sure they know how adored they are. I see so clearly the invaluable gift they are to me and everyone they know. When any one of my six children walk into the room, I light up with genuine joy. It's the same for all of them, no difference. The fact that some are biological and some are adopted isn't a factor.

About a year after our first child was born, we began to ask the Lord how we could serve the needy. We found our devotion times brought two key verses: first, "God sets the lonely in families" (Psalm 68:6), and second, "By wisdom a house is built and through understanding it is established; through knowledge its rooms are filled with rare and beautiful treasures" (Proverbs 24:3–4).

The culmination of seeking God for direction led us to open our home to pregnant women in need, and New Beginnings

Home was established. The first week we opened brought one new woman each day for six days. Suddenly, our rooms were filled with rare and beautiful treasures.

That papa's heart has carried over into the ways I interact with the young women we serve. Many have never experienced a father who was worthy of their trust. I so deeply want these women to taste and see that God is good—and that starts with my example. From there, they will hopefully see their own value, too. All I can do is try my best to treat them in a way that communicates that. Oh, how I pray they will one day see themselves as the treasures they are!

I recall a time when one young woman was found hiding out during the birthday party we were throwing to celebrate her, simply because she was overcome with emotion. No one in her entire life had ever celebrated the day she was born. It brings tears to my eyes even now. She soon joined in the fun, and we had a nice party.

Another time, my wife, Debi, and I had gone off on a much-needed dinner date. Upon returning home, we found the fire department extinguishing a grease fire in

the kitchen that started because a resident left a burner on. The resident was sobbing, overwhelmed with shame and condemnation. When I saw that, I reached up on the soot-covered wall and wrote out, "I still love you." We've stayed in touch over the years, and she says she will never forget that night.

Showing love, grace, and encouragement is the definition of a papa. I have such fond memories growing up alongside my identical twin brother with the affection and attention of our dad, whom we called Papa. And so, the title brings me immense gratitude: in 40 years, over 600 women in our care, many of their children, and my own seven grandchildren have called on me by the name Papa.

I've taken what my own papa modeled for me and what Father God has taught me and just do my best. I don't always get it right, but I always try. I just hope anyone who has ever called me Papa knows I love them.

53

FATHER DAVID MULHOLLAND

Father Dave Mulholland grew up in Tacoma, Washington. He attended Washington State University and practiced law until the persistent call to become a priest wouldn't let go of his heart. In addition to loving his role as pastor of Saint Patrick's church, he continues to fan the flame of his first love: the WSU Cougars!

The Priest as a Spiritual Father

One Sunday after Mass, a dad with four little ones pulling and tugging him out the doors of the church smiled at me and said, "Father David, I sometimes envy you; you don't have to be wrangled by kids all the time like me!"

"You are mistaken, friend," I quickly said to him as people were milling about. "I have a thousand kids wrangling me all the time!" And immediately his smile widened and he added a thumbs up!

It's so true. Any pastor knows deep down he is a father to many. When a priest is ordained, one of the first things that strikes the heart—and it happens right on ordination day—is that people start calling you "Father." At first it sounds odd, and it can even feel a bit uncomfortable. But soon you begin to live that reality as ministry takes hold in your life. For God gives each priest the capacity to receive the beautiful charism to be a spiritual father, a dad to many.

"Christ beside me,
Christ before me,
Christ behind me,
Christ within me,
Christ beneath me,
Christ above me."

– Saint Patrick

All a pastor's parishioners, young, old, and in between, are his spiritual children. More precisely, he is entrusted with the care of souls within the entire parish boundary. Everyone is important who lives in the parish, even those who are not Catholic. A good pastor faithfully prays for all his spiritual children close by: Catholic, Protestant, Muslim, Jewish, atheist, and agnostic alike. Each one is commended to God's good care every day by their spiritual father.

It's obvious that prayer for your children is one of the most important tasks of a spiritual father. So is teaching, guiding, protecting, and challenging one's children. We know all good fathers are called to do this. And then, there's blessing: a spiritual father imparts God's blessing upon his children so they can be open to all the spiritual graces that flow from the Lord for our healing, our joy, and our happiness. A priest does this often, but so too should all fathers. All fathers are called to be spiritual leaders in their families and to bless them often!

The Lord Jesus said: "Whoever has seen me has seen the Father" (John 14:9). A priest acts in the person of Christ, and in doing so, he helps to make the presence of the Father, through Christ, a reality in people's lives. One of the most important spiritual roles for a father is to confirm and affirm their children's identity as God's beloved ones.

For me, reminding my "children" they are beloved sons and daughters of the Father is a task I never tire of. Our modern world tells us to find our identity in any number of things, like our ethnicity, race, sexuality, gender, political ideologies, et cetera. But our true identity is so simple: we are beloved ones of God! Whether young or old, we constantly need to be reminded of this truth. And I love to do the reminding. Whether it's at a baptism, a talk or retreat, or in my preaching, I feel this is an important responsibility for me as a spiritual father.

In fact, just before writing these words, I had the joy of praying with and commending a "beloved one" to God her Father as she neared the end of a very long and good life. From me she received the anointing of the sick, a blessing, a prayer, and a kiss on the forehead as my spiritual daughter. Her quiet, simple response? "Thank you, Father." Words that warm my heart every time!

Praise be to Jesus Christ.

"Be who God meant you to be
and you will set the world on fire."
– St. Catherine of Siena

54

BRIAN KRANICK

Brian Kranick has written two books—*Burning Bush, Burning Hearts: Exodus as Paradigm of the Gospel*, and his latest commentary—*Exodus and the Apocalypse: A Brief Typological Inquiry*. Brian has a master's degree in System-

atic Theology from Christendom College, and spent years working as an analyst in the Intelligence Community. He currently resides in the Pacific Northwest with his wife, three children, and their dog.

My father died when I was five years old. I don't have many memories of him, just a few brief flashbacks etched into my mind. I remember playing a game with him chasing me around the dining room table. I remember falling asleep on his shoulder as he carried me upstairs to bed. I recall a strange breathing device he had in the hospital after he was diagnosed with cancer. I think about my dad often and pray for him every morning. I miss my dad, even though I never really knew him. In those few brief years I knew him, he had a dramatic impact on my life. Even after all these years and decades, his loss affects me. I am grateful I had a father for those formative years. It makes me think of the great importance of fatherhood. Dads mean everything to their children, and fatherhood is such immense responsibility that I'm amazed that God entrusts us with these little human beings.

As it turns out, I became a father as well. I have three amazing daughters. I love fatherhood, and I love my kids, even though being a parent is such an exhausting undertaking. It is worth it. I can't imagine the trials and tribulations my mom went through as a single mom to three young kids. Yet, she persevered as a saintly, wonderful mother.

Fatherhood reminds me that Jesus taught us to call God "our Father." God is a father. In seeing the best of our fathers and fatherhood, we see small glimpses into who God really is. God is a loving dad. Our loving dads reflect God, who is our Father. The Trinity is a loving family relationship. God is the Father, God is the Son, God is the Holy Spirit. God the Father eternally begat God the Son, and from the love of the Father and the Son eternally proceeds the person of the Holy Spirit.

To be a good father is to imitate the divine. Perhaps this is why fatherhood is of the utmost importance in our lives. Even if we're not always aware of the reason, maybe this is why we innately strive to be good fathers—we're trying to be like our Father in Heaven. Being a good dad is a big deal. And if you are a dad, above all else, fatherhood is your vocation.

55

RANDY MOON

Randy has been married to his wife, Jan, for 22 years and describes himself as a father, teacher, coach, and friend. He loves God and he loves kids, and he has given his life to these noble endeavors by serving his family, teaching, and coaching. He has been at it for decades, with no end in sight.

בְּרוּךָ אַתָּה יְיָ

Barukh atah Adonai

Blessed are you, Lord

אֱלֹהֵינוּ מֶלֶךָ הָעוֹלָם

Eloheinu, melekh ha'olam

our God, sovereign of the universe

אֲשֶׁר קִדְּשָׁנוּ בְּמִצְוֹתָיו

asher kid'shanu b'mitz'votav

Who has sanctified us with His commandments

וְרָצָה בָנוּ

v'ratzah vanu

and has been pleased with us

וְשַׁבָּת קָדְשׁוֹ

v'shabat kad'sho

and your holy Shabbat

בְּאַהֲבָה וּבְרָצוֹן הִנְחִילָנוּ

b'ahavah uv'ratzon hin'chilanu

you have lovingly and willingly given us as an inheritance

זִכָּרוֹן לְמַעֲשֵׂה בְרֵאשִׁית

zikaron l'ma'aseih v'rei'shit

in memory of the work of creation

כִּי הוּא יוֹם תְּחִלָּה

ki hu yom t'chilah

because it is the first day

שֶׁדָּק יֵאַרְקְמִל
l'mik'ra'ei kodesh
of our holy assemblies

הְשָׁדָק תַּבַּשׁוּ
v'shabat kad'sh'kha
and Your holy Shabbat

סיָרְצַּמ תַּאיצִיל רֶכָז
zeikher litzi'at Mitz'rayim
in memory of the exodus from Egypt

וּנְתַּלְחִנְה וֹצָרְבוּ הָבַהְאַב
b'ahavah uv'ratzon hin'chal'tanu.
you have lovingly and willingly given us
for an inheritance

תָרְחָב וּנָב יִכ.
ki vanu vachar'ta
because You have chosen us

יְי הָתַאַ דוּרָב
Barukh atah Adonai
Blessed are you,

סיַמַעָה לָכְמ.תְּשָׁדָק וּנָתוֹאְו
v'otanu kidash'ta mikol ha'amim
and made us holy from all peoples

נֵמָא :תָבַּשַׁה שֵׁדָקְמ
m'kadeish hashabat. Amein.
who sanctifies Shabbat. Amen.

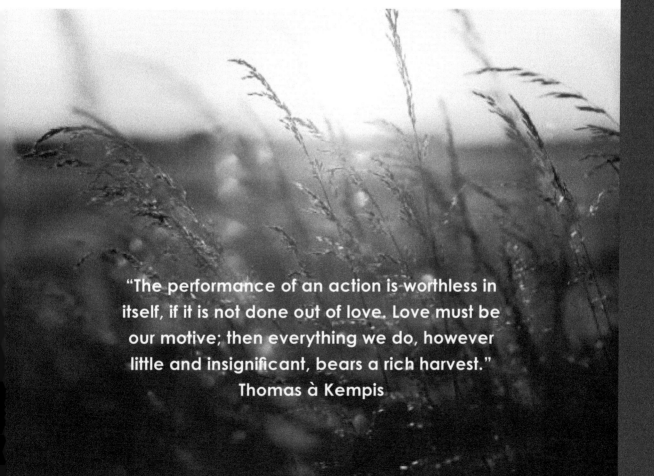

"The performance of an action is worthless in itself, if it is not done out of love. Love must be our motive; then everything we do, however little and insignificant, bears a rich harvest."
Thomas à Kempis

When our children were growing up, every Friday night, we would have a blessing. After our family sat down to a nice dinner, I would go around the table and bless all the family members. I would start with all the kids, anointing each head with oil, blessing them and my wife. The main blessing I would say was in Hebrew: "*Baruch Atah Adonai, Eloheinu Melech ha'olam, sh'hecheyanu, v'kiyemanu, v'higianu la'zman hazeh.*" In English, that means, "Blessed are You, God, Ruler of the universe, who has given us life and sustained us and enabled us to reach this season."

This was our routine for quite a while, until suddenly, the kids wanted to bless my wife, Jan, and me too. This was a precious, endearing request. My children would take turns blessing us. Initially, some had to stand on a chair so they could reach our foreheads. These reciprocal blessings continued and became the new expanded tradition each week.

One time, our youngest child wanted to bless us too. He was six or seven years old at the time and had never participated before. He went around the table and blessed each brother and sister by name. He was saying all kinds of things for them and my wife. Finally, he arrived at me, climbed up on the chair… and was silent. All our heads were bowed, and around the 20-second mark, I was thinking, *Wow! This must be something special!*

Then, after 10 more seconds, he announced, "I got nothing!"

We laughed so hard. It was just precious.

I wish I knew more Hebrew, and this prayer tradition inspires me to go deeper in this learning. When I retire from teaching, I would like to learn it.

Inevitably, time has marched on, and it is harder and harder to continue this Friday tradition. Our youngest is now 17 years old, and carving out family time has become one of the trickiest things to do. On Friday nights now, our kids are busy playing sports or hanging out with friends. Yet although it looks different, and it may not always be on a Friday, I still try to find them and pray before bed, as well as when they are already asleep. This tradition is special because after not having had the best example of a father growing up, my wife and I wanted to make sure God's blessing through me, their earthly father, would remind them they belong to Someone.

I won't ever stop blessing them and praying for them. I miss the simpler times, those days where consistency and routine brought structure in prayer and life. But I also am thankful for these days, where they are ready to launch into the world. I am excited for them and confident that God Himself will be faithful in continuing to bless them.

"When you die, you take nothing from earth with you, and the main thing you leave behind is the legacy of how well you loved."

– Cheryl Smith

The traditional family is rebeliion
against the modern world.

56

JUAN LEZCANO

Juan and Karen Lezcano have been married for 43 years, and have nine adult children and 14 grandchildren. Juan and Karen are members of the Secular Franciscan Order and parishioners at St. Vincent de Paul Parish in Federal Way, Washington, where Juan serves as a parish deacon.

In 1983, our family moved to Japan with the U.S. Army. At the time, our family consisted of my wife, Karen, who was pregnant with Anthony (born two months after our arrival in Japan), Elizabeth, age three, and Christopher, age 10 months. Very soon after arriving at Camp Zama, Karen and I became involved with Mother Saint Teresa of Calcutta's Missionary Sisters of Charity, who ministered to unwed mothers. This ministry served women who had chosen not to have an abortion.

Through our involvement with the Missionaries of Charity, we were introduced to the work of the Missionary Brothers of Charity, their male counterpart. The brothers' ministry was to homeless men in the Roppongi District, a suburb of Tokyo. Since my days in the seminary, I had developed a yearly habit of going on retreat, but since I was new to Japan, Sr. Ruth, the superior of the Missionary Sisters of Charity in Japan, arranged for me to make a week retreat with the Missionary Brothers of Charity. As a part of my retreat, I was able to spend time with the brothers ministering to the homeless, which led me to spending most of my free time traveling to the Roppongi District, a 30-minute train ride, to serve there as well.

During this time, Karen was not only staying at home with and caring for our newborn, our toddler, and our three-year-old, but she was now pregnant with our fourth child (Susan).

In 1994, we received word that Mother Teresa was coming to Japan to visit her communities. At the encouragement of Sr. Ruth, our base commander sent a formal invitation to Mother Teresa to visit Camp Zama and speak to our military families on the sanctity of life, to which she responded that she would be very happy to visit our community while in Japan.

In early November, she arrived at Camp Zama. Three of us were tasked with taking care of Mother Teresa, prior to her talk to the military community, which now included the Navy, Marines, and Air Force communities nearby. Mother Teresa was flown by helicopter from Tokyo to Camp Zama, and brought to the Chapel to have dinner, prior to meeting dignitaries and speaking to the military community assembled at the Camp Zama High School Auditorium.

The three of who had been charged with taking care of Mother Teresa, her traveling companion, and Sr. Ruth prepared the room and proceeded to bring

"Thank God ahead of time.
God knows best, and, while we'll still hope for a favorable surprise, we can hardly do better than not only being resigned to whatever God permits but even beforehand to thank Him for His mercifully loving designs."

- Solanus Casey

them their meal. It was at this time that Sr. Ruth introduced me to Mother Teresa, sharing with her the work I had been doing and the time I had spent to support the work of the ministries to unwed mothers and the homeless. Even with four children at home, including a newborn, I was still spending many hours—and sometimes even whole weeks—away from home.

After Mother Teresa had listened to Sr. Ruth for a considerable length of time, she motioned me to come closer to her. She looked me in the eyes and with a gentle but stern voice, she said:

"It is the mission and work of the Missionary Sisters and Brothers of Charity to take care of the unwed mothers, the homeless men, and those in need. And it is your *mission and responsibility to support and take care of your wife and your children. Later in life God will call you to do the works of charity and mercy."*

This was a lesson I clearly needed to learn and have never forgotten.

Foster Father by Tianna Williams
www.sacredartbytianna.com

About the Authors

ANGELA CONNELLY

Angela began the Crowded Table series with her first book, *The Crowded Table: The Brave and Beautiful Choice to Mother Many* (2022). She is a graduate of Thomas Aquinas College, where she is now a member of the Board of Governors. Angela's passions are her family, faith, growing flowers, and serving local and national nonprofits focusing on women, children, and fighting homelessness. She and her husband live in the Pacific Northwest, where they have raised their nine rowdy children and now enjoy their five granddaughters.

MEGAN MCDANIEL

Megan holds a master's degree in social work, and serves as a professional Social Worker providing counseling to children, adults, and their families for over 25 years. She is passionate about the topics of fatherhood, families, and her faith, and enjoys writing about all of these and especially about the important ways in which they intersect.

MANOLA SECAIRA

Manola is a wife, a mom, and a dentist, who was born and raised in Guatemala. She and her husband currently reside in Washington State and have eight children who are now forming families of their own.

CPSIA information can be obtained
at www.ICGtesting.com
Printed in the USA
JSHW070952220623
43216JS00001B/4